CHIPPEWA FALLS
World War II Hero
Harry W. Kramer

JOHN E. KINVILLE

THE
History
PRESS

Published by The History Press
Charleston, SC
www.historypress.com

Copyright © 2023 by John E. Kinville
All rights reserved

Front cover, top right: Envelope, address and cancellation stamp, May 14, 1941. *Author's collection. Center left*: Stationery from the USS *California*, 1940. *Author's collection. Bottom right*: Envelope, address and cancellation stamp, 1941. *Author's collection. Bottom left*: Envelope and cancellation stamp, May 11, 1940. *Author's collection.*
Back cover, top: Letter from Harry to Jack Selden, May 6, 1940. *Author's collection. Center*: "Aloha, Harry," 1940. Author's collection.

First published 2023

Manufactured in the United States

ISBN 9781467152495

Library of Congress Control Number: 2022949525

*For Michael, Evelyne, Earl, David, Barbara,
Annie and the rest of the Kramer family.*

CONTENTS

Contents

PREFACE

So, what made me decide to write a book on a sailor named Harry Wellington Kramer? The answer to that question requires context. Even though I was born in Michigan, I have always considered myself a "Chippewa kid." My parents, raised in Eau Claire, moved to Chippewa Falls when I was an infant. I graduated from Chippewa Falls High School in 1997 and went on to earn a teaching degree from the University of Wisconsin–Eau Claire. Ironically, my first and only teaching job has been at my high school alma mater, where I have taught social studies for nearly twenty years.

During my first year of teaching, in 2003, my principals, James Sauter and Rebecca Davis, invited me to be part of a special committee of school officials and community members charged with designing a military tribute to honor our school's fallen soldiers. They had recognized the need for one. I immediately and excitedly accepted his invitation. By the end of our work, a memorial consisting of forty engraved names, affixed to a large, rectangular wooden plaque, was erected to honor the identified alumni who died while serving in the military.

Each time I stopped to read their names, I found myself wanting to know more. In 2009, a colleague, Amanda Hill-Hable, and I founded a school club called Flags 4 the Fallen. The plan was for student volunteers to connect with our school's military past by researching the personal, historical, geographical and cultural details connected to each of the fallen. The information uncovered would be used to plan site visits to honor their service.

Over the years, we have watched club members develop deep connections with our fallen heroes. We observed McKayla Streit leave a personal letter and an engraved stone with a heart at the grave of U.S. Army corporal John T. Christie in Gettysburg National Cemetery. We joined our heads in solemn respect at the Vietnam Veterans Memorial in Washington, D.C., as Andrew Gehl offered an American flag in the memory of air force major Wilbur A. Skaar. We stood at proud attention in a small Wisconsin town cemetery as Nicole Johnson played taps on her trumpet, honoring the birthday of marine PFC Frederick "Fritz" Bungartz. These profound moments constitute only a small sampling of the meaningful connections Flags 4 the Fallen has fostered.

It wasn't until 2012 that Mariah Meyers, a student researcher, rediscovered information that one of our fallen had been lost at Pearl Harbor, on December 7, 1941. The man's name was Harry Wellington Kramer. He was killed while serving on the USS *California* and was laid to rest in Hawaii, at the National Memorial Cemetery of the Pacific. Everyone was stunned, as no one had ever heard of him. A phone call to our city's American Legion organization confirmed the finding, as they informed us that Post No. 77 was partially named after him.

It was universally believed by our students that Flags 4 the Fallen needed to travel to Pearl Harbor to visit our fallen sailor. The tour was scheduled for the summer of 2013. With Mariah leading the way, club members shifted into in-depth genealogy research in order to identify surviving relatives. Since Harry died a bachelor and had no children of his own, his closest surviving relatives were nieces and nephews. One niece, Evelyne, still resided in western Wisconsin and agreed to meet with us.

On behalf of herself and her surviving siblings, Gerald, David, Earl and Barbara, Evelyne gave us a large box that contained everything they had on Uncle Harry Kramer. The trove included everything from baby pictures, report cards and handwritten letters to navy photographs, Hawaiian mementos and ephemera from the USS *California*. Also included were the Asiatic and Pacific Defense medal, the American Defense medal, the Victory in World War medal and the Purple Heart. The box also contained a neatly folded American flag, similar to those used to drape caskets, as well as a wooden plaque in the shape of a shield, which had once prominently adorned the halls of Harry Wellington Kramer's old high school. One student asked, "Why isn't that still hanging in the school?"

At the very bottom of the box was an ornate wooden photo album from the 1940s. Each page contained either photographs, postcards or handwritten

Sampling of letters Harry Wellington Kramer sent home from his time in the U.S. Navy, 2022. *Author's collection.*

letters. A total of thirty-three personal letters between Harry and his friends and family were neatly housed in their original envelopes. Carefully, we read and documented each.

What became apparent to the club was that Harry Wellington Kramer was truly a unique individual. His letters revealed a young man who was likable, thoughtful, excitable and devout—an "old soul" who wasn't all that far removed from high school. He enjoyed eating large amounts of food, drank a lot of Coca-Cola and hoped to one day own a pet cat. He spent his liberty time sightseeing, reading religious books, meeting people connected to his faith and spending quality time with a handful of distant relatives living in Southern California.

Since our connection with Evelyne began, Flags 4 the Fallen students have visited Harry's grave in 2013 and again in 2017. During the club's most recent visit to Pearl Harbor, I stood at Harry's grave and made two promises to him: first, that I would help the club establish a tribute to Harry's service and sacrifice in the high school, and second, that I would one day write a book about his life and experiences. As a historian, I have found that too often, we analyze military moments through body count totals and the battlefront leaders who won or lost. On December 7, 1941, 2,403 Americans were killed, both servicemembers and civilians.[1] Each victim was a unique soul who was rendered unable to fulfill their life's dreams and aspirations. Each left behind a slew of grieving community members and close friends and dear family. The following pages will tell the story of one such sailor.

ACKNOWLEDGEMENTS

This book would not have been possible without the support of the National Archives at St. Louis, Missouri; the National Archives at College Park, Maryland; the Wisconsin State Historical Society; the Chippewa County Historical Society; the Chippewa County Genealogy Society; the Chippewa Valley Museum; the Chippewa Falls Public Library; the *Chippewa Herald*; and the National World War II Museum in New Orleans, Louisiana.

Special thanks to John Rodrigue and Zoe Ames at The History Press, for believing in the project; Alex Daverede at History Hub, for answering my obscure questions; and the office of United States Senator Tammy Baldwin, for expediting the release of Harry Kramer's official military personnel file.

Without my Kickstarter.com project investors, I wouldn't have had the necessary financial resources to finish the project. They include: Suzanne Kent, Nate Henderson, Tristi Crawford, Eric and Lora Sinclair, Jim and Nina Kramer, Earl Kramer and Mary Sommermeyer, Barbara Kramer, Mark and Lori Isaacson, Dana Miller, Jacob Hyde, Abbie and Will Steiger, Cody James Zimmerman, Monica Jones, Dawn Kloss, Trenton Smith, Madame Anne Keller, Eugene and Keelyn Huettel, Travis Tainter, Kate Lapp, CJ Sailey, Chad Bormann, Patti Norquist, Nick Zutter, Logan Erickson, Dennis Fehr, State Senator Jesse James, Dawn Paschal, Jean Selden, Van Isaacson, Sheena Harings, Melissa Shear, Dylan Helwig, Evan Dillman, Jason Hicks, Roger and Sheila Thompson, Isaac Solberg, Matt and Leya Hoy, Jessi Hoy Peterson, Christopher Davis, Katie DeWitt, Tiffany Woghan, Matthew

Klund, Kalene Prentice, Dana Mercier, Stacy Shuda, Mike Torres, Jason Bejin, Mandy Miller, Mikayla DuBois, Connor Lehmann, Michael Houle and Joe Niese.

As a proud product of Wisconsin's public education system, I want to recognize the outstanding teachers, professors and support staff of the Chippewa Falls Area Unified School District, the University of Wisconsin–Eau Claire and the University of Wisconsin–River Falls. In particular, I would like to thank Mark Isaacson, Darrin Ekern, Tom Frederick, Anne Keller, James Sauter, Rebecca Davis, Oscar Chamberlain, James Oberly, Selika Ducksworth-Lawton, Jane Pederson, Roger Tlusty and Kurt Leichtle.

I also want to highlight the encouragement I have received from numerous others, including David Martineau, Jason Bobb, Amanda Hill-Hable, Steve Wisner, Lisa Hable, Larry Dittner, Victor Cable, Anya Schreiner, Michelle Golden and the late Ned Hanson.

The patience and support bestowed on me by my family has been incredible, including my parents, John and Carolyn Kinville; my sons, Jack and Jonathan; my daughter, Savannah; and my four cats, Huey, Ghost, Garfield and Ms. Pacman. And most of all, my wife, Kara; she has been nothing short of extraordinary.

Lastly, I want to extend my sincerest gratitude to Harry's family, including his nieces and nephews, Carl, Gerald, David, Earl, Evelyne and Barbara Kramer, as well as his great-niece Annie Kramer and his great-great-nephew Michael Kramer. Without their insight and support, much of the context for this book would not have been possible. In particular, it's the patience, decency, persistence and resolve of Evelyne Yungerberg, Harry's niece, that have been so instrumental to this book. Despite the recent loss of her husband, John, and her older brother David, Evelyne always made time for my inquiries. I will forever be grateful for her strength and friendship.

INTRODUCTION

O n Tuesday, March 31, 1942, Chippewa Falls Senior High School
played host to a memorial program in honor of Harry Wellington
Kramer, the first Chippewa County man to lose his life in what
would later be known as World War II. Because he was killed on December
7, 1941, at Pearl Harbor, details surrounding Harry's death were still largely
unknown. In the three months and twenty-four days since the U.S. Navy
confirmed Harry's death, there had been no official word on whether his
body had been recovered. Up until a week prior, his ship, the USS *California*,
had still been partially submerged, resting on the harbor's forty-foot bottom.
Harry's family, friends and community were left with numerous unanswered
questions, not knowing when or if those answers would ever come. Since the
country was now at war on multiple fronts, details surrounding December 7
would take years, and even decades, to be fully understood.[2]

But on this solemn day, students, staff and select community members
gathered to pay tribute to one of their own. Just four years earlier, Harry
had been walking these halls. As the auditorium seats filled up, a small group
of students escorted Harry's parents, Ralph and Eva Kramer, to their front-
row seats. The program was designed to not only memorialize Harry but
also honor the parents who had raised a son of impeccable character and
reputation.[3]

The program opened with a standing ovation, and as the high school
band played their rendition of "My Country, 'Tis of Thee," the crowd
joined in. Student senior class president Bill Rodiger then led the Pledge of

Postcard featuring the former Chippewa Falls Senior High School in the city's downtown, circa 1920. *Author's collection.*

Allegiance, followed by the school band's performance of "The Stars and Stripes Forever."[4] High school principal Howard M. Lyon paid tribute to Harry's memory and implored everyone to "rededicate ourselves to things for which Harry always stood." Faculty member Grace Walsh spoke next, sharing her own remembrances of Harry and concluding by reading a prewritten statement on behalf of Harry's parents, neither of whom was in an emotional position to read it themselves. The theme of their letter was to urge the boys and girls of the school "to build their lives upon a foundation of high ideals," just as Harry had. The Kramers were then introduced to the crowd, as a group of female students presented Harry's mother with a corsage bouquet, symbolizing American motherhood. A wooden plaque in the shape of a shield, which included Harry's name and designation in the U.S. Navy, was also shown to the grieving parents. The principal assured them that Harry's memory would never be forgotten and that the tribute would be prominently displayed in the halls of the school.[5] The plaque read:

In Memory of
Harry Kramer
Born Nov. 10, 1919
Killed at Pearl Harbor—December 7, 1941
Class of 1938[6]

Harry W. Kramer

Harry W. Kramer Memorial Held

Chippewa Falls High School Students Honor City's First War Casualty.

Newspaper headline covering the Harry W. Kramer Memorial at Chippewa Falls High School, March 31, 1942. *Author's collection.*

After a senior student, Joe Mandelert, read the poem "Seeds of Disillusionment," Principal Lyon read the condolence letters Ralph and Eva had received from both the captain of the USS *California* and the secretary of the United States Navy. Mayor John Zesiger spoke next about Harry's memory and legacy, while senior class president Bill Rodiger finished with a call for the entire student body to take a more active part in the nation's war effort, especially in the area of civilian defense. The program concluded with a plethora of musical numbers, including student Keith LaGesse singing "I Am an American," the boys' quartet performing "Remember Pearl Harbor" and the audience collectively chorusing the "Star-Spangled Banner."[7]

Despite the enormity of the pain and anguish Ralph and Eva continued to feel over the loss of their youngest son, they were grateful and deeply moved by the program held at his alma mater. The *Chippewa Herald-Telegram* published their "card of thanks":

We wish to take this opportunity to express our thanks for the time and effort given by the Mayor, the Board of Education, the Senior High School Faculty, the Student Body, and others who sponsored the Memorial Service in honor of our son, Harry W. Kramer, who lost his life at Pearl Harbor. It was a high tribute to a worthy son of this city, and we his parents, deeply appreciate it.

Mr. and Mrs. Ralph B. Kramer[8]

In the days, months and years after Harry's death, family, friends and community members were inspired by his sacrifice to help support the war effort wherever they could. Local students raised money in schools, and residents flocked to purchase war bonds. Nationally, workers began paying record-high income taxes to the government, while women skillfully and successfully filled vacated industrial jobs left by men off to war.

America's collective resolve during this time earned everyone living in it the moniker "the Greatest Generation," derived from the title of a book written by NBC journalist Tom Brokaw. This generation has been generally defined as people born from 1901 to 1927. Each was shaped by the impact of the stock market crash of 1929, the Great Depression that ensued and their domestic or foreign participation in World War II.[9] But just as time inevitably marches on, so do the challenges of people living in subsequent generations; their focus has turned to the Cold War, the civil rights movement, the Vietnam War, women's rights, nuclear proliferation, the environmental movement, the war on terrorism and many other issues in between.

Each day, untold numbers of citizens from the Greatest Generation pass away. As of this writing, the youngest member of that generation is ninety-six years of age. As one would expect, the broad social memory of monumental historical events—such as the attack on Pearl Harbor—remains, but the personalization of such moments gets lost over time. Even the wooden plaque, so proudly unveiled at the 1942 memorial program, had disappeared from the halls of Harry's alma mater. As students and staff transitioned to a newly constructed high school on the city's west hill, the plaque was unceremoniously returned to the family in the mid-1960s. Eventually, the old downtown high school, including what was left of a tribute wall listing all the names of those who served and died in World War II, was demolished in 1963. No replacement memorial to Harry, or the others, was erected.

Today, in Chippewa Falls, there are few surviving residents who personally remember Harry Kramer. Some remember him well. Others, due to their young age at the time, remember only snippets. Mostly, people have not heard of him. In order to change this trajectory, I present in this book Harry's story through the letters he exchanged with friends and relatives while in the navy. I have supplemented these with the key global happenings that his parents, Ralph and Eva, would have read about in the *Chippewa Herald-Telegram*. My intention is to supply readers with the most comprehensive view of the lead-up to the attack on Pearl Harbor, from the people who actually lived it firsthand. This book is not meant to be an all-inclusive retrospective on the lead-up to World War II but rather a window into the reported stories read by the actual people in this book. As a result, numerous topics of popular interest to World War II enthusiasts don't surface much, including the Holocaust and various speculations and debates surrounding the Pearl Harbor attack.

The following pages contain the transcriptions, either partial or in full, of thirty-three letters exchanged between Harry Kramer and his mother, Eva; his father, Ralph; his friend Jack Selden; and Jack's mother, Jessie Selden. These letters were written between February 1940 and November 1941, while Harry was serving in the U.S. Navy—all but three by Harry himself. Supplementing these letters is a wide variety of ancillary research material pertaining to the people, places and events mentioned throughout. Harry visited a lot of locations, met numerous individuals and referenced a wide array of topics and people back in his hometown. Using a combination of sources, including genealogical archives, newspapers, city directories, United States Census records, historical books and numerous Internet websites, each personal letter has been explained and clarified to provide context for the reader.

Most importantly, the following pages have been structured to supply two distinct perspectives leading up to the attack on Pearl Harbor. The first is Harry's, forged through his letters, which provide a window into the world of prewar navy life. However, these would have been subject to the restrictions of a military censor. As a result, Harry would have avoided discussing specific navy information, ship movements and details pertaining to global affairs. This limits both readers' and historians' ability to get a complete view of the experiences Harry and of sailors like him. The second perspective is that of Harry's family, as they would have consumed a daily dose of newspaper stories chronicling the developing conflicts around the world. Ralph and Robert Kramer, in particular, possessed a strong appetite for national and international affairs. In order to encapsulate this important perspective, newspaper accounts from their hometown newspaper, once titled the *Chippewa Herald-Telegram*, have been painstakingly incorporated to supplement the timeline provided by the letters. The end goal of this method is to give a comprehensive view, through the eyes of the Kramer family and the Chippewa Falls community, into one of the most infamous events in American history. This is Harry's story.

PART I

The Kramer Family

Chapter 1

FAMILY ROOTS IN NORTHWESTERN WISCONSIN

In Eau Claire, Wisconsin, on Wednesday, March 30, 1910, Harry
Wellington Kramer's parents, Ralph Buhlen Kramer and Eva
(pronounced "*eave*-a") Lazelle Webb, united in marriage in the two-
story east side home of Eva's aunt Annabelle Bonnell. The ceremony, held at
1046 Barland Street, was portrayed in the Eau Claire newspaper as "one of
the prettiest weddings of the present season." At six o'clock in the evening,
the bridal party descended from the second floor to the sound of Richard
Wagner's traditional "Here Comes the Bride," played on the piano by the
Bonnells' young daughter, Edna.[10] The thirty-year-old bride was "beautifully
gowned in soft white material," as she held a full bouquet of white roses. Her
twenty-five-year-old groom was standing on the first floor, in the northeast
corner of the parlor room, wearing a suit of "conventional black."[11] One
guest remembered that as the pair first locked eyes when Eva reached the
base of the staircase, the couple "looked at each other as if their hearts were
within their eyes."[12] As the bride and groom joined hands in front of a large
decorative "bank of palms," a pastor from Bethel Baptist Church united
them in a "brief, but beautiful service." The ring, which had been "hidden
among the petals of a beautiful, singular white rose," was brought forward
to symbolize and sanctify their union. Immediately following the ceremony,
the newlyweds ate a "bountiful wedding dinner" and unwrapped "many
beautiful and useful presents" with family and friends.[13]

After a honeymoon split between Chicago and Duluth, the newlyweds
packed up their belongings and uprooted to Devils Lake, North Dakota,

Thirty-year-old Eva Kramer in her wedding dress, circa 1910. *Author's collection.*

population just over 5,100. Ralph had been working as a traveling dry goods salesman for the F.A. Patrick Dry Goods Company.[14] The wholesale company, based in a seven-story building in Duluth, specialized in ready-to-wear woolen clothing made from mackinaw cloth. This heavy, dense and water-repellant woolen material had become trendy in the United States. Having originated with Canadian frontiersmen, the fabric had been made famous by American lumberjacks in the Upper Midwest. Overcoats and blankets were most in demand and routinely sold in bright colors and loud patterns, including the quintessential red-and-black checkered plaid design.[15]

Ralph's career as a traveling salesman required that he spend an inordinate amount of time away from his new wife. Eva, meanwhile, was no stranger to the demands of being married to a traveling salesman. She had once operated her own milliner's shop in Tomah, Wisconsin, where she cultivated a reputation for being a gifted women's hatmaker. Eva would have conversed with numerous salesmen coming in and out of the shop. Presumably, this is how Eva had Ralph first met.[16]

In many ways, the two might have seemed an unlikely pairing. Eva was short in stature, introverted and meek, whereas Ralph was tall, sociable and possessed of a vivacious "gift of gab." Eva didn't use tobacco of any kind and spent her downtime reading religious materials, while Ralph chain-smoked cigarettes and preferred reading newspapers and keeping up on current events. As it so happened, the two ended up complementing each other well.[17]

After her marriage, Eva transitioned to life as a homemaker as she settled into the couple's house at 511 Sixth Street in Devils Lake. There, she became active in the city's First Methodist Church and prepared for the arrival of their first child.[18] On February 13, 1911, Eva gave birth to a son, Robert Lincoln Kramer. As Abraham Lincoln had been born one day earlier, on February 12, Ralph proposed that they honor the American icon by giving their son his name.[19]

Despite Ralph and Eva's recent successes and marital happiness, both envisioned that one day, they could move back to the Chippewa River Valley. Ralph, whose father had also worked as a salesman, was born in 1884 in Eau (pronounced "O") Claire. The former lumber boom city still dominated the economic and cultural landscape of western Wisconsin. At eighteen thousand residents, Eau Claire had maintained over three times the population of Devils Lake and was beginning to grow again at a feverish pace. The large prevalence of ethnic Germans also made the area popular for families like the Kramers.[20]

By contrast, Eva had been raised in the sparsity of a rural township named Eagle Point, situated some twenty-five miles north of Eau Claire and just eight miles north of Chippewa Falls. Eva was born, in 1879, into a farming family of largely English heritage. After the birth of Robert and because Ralph was always on the road, the lonely Eva left North Dakota to spend the summer with her family and friends in Chippewa Falls.[21]

Chapter 2

A SECOND SON BORN IN EAU CLAIRE

In the spring of 1919, Ralph, Eva and Robert, now seven, moved into a two-story home in Eau Claire. Ralph had since obtained a more lucrative job as a traveling salesman for the Chicago-based Marshall Field and Company. This wholesaler was known for its quality dry good products, ranging from fabric and clothing to jewelry and furniture.

In addition to the family's large home on Oxford Avenue, on the city's trendy west side, Ralph purchased a brand-new Studebaker automobile.[22] All of these changes were precipitated by the fact that the couple had been preparing for the arrival of a second child. The day they moved into their new home, on May 1, Eva was just beginning her third month of pregnancy.[23]

On November 10, 1919, an unseasonably warm, fifty-eight-degree Monday, the Kramers welcomed their second son.[24] Forty-year-old Eva, knowing that this was likely the last child she would conceive, decided the boy's name ought to include a tribute to her father, Wellington Webb. Thus, Harry Wellington Kramer arrived at Luther Hospital in Eau Claire.[25] The family of four returned home with an eagerness to grow and share their futures together.

But within a year or so after Harry's birth, Ralph quit his job with Marshall Field and Company. Family lore recounts an "argument" he had with someone over sales routes, which led to the untimely separation. The strong-willed Ralph, for better or for worse, was not known to back down from a conflict. With finances strained, Ralph sold their home, as well as the Studebaker he so enjoyed. The family moved into a nearby rental property and purchased an older and less reliable vehicle.[26]

Two-year old Harry, 1921. *Author's collection.*

Ralph's attempts to find a similarly paying job proved difficult. While Eva and the children lived in Eau Claire, Ralph purchased and operated a restaurant in Greenwood, located some sixty miles to the east. To no financial avail, Ralph jettisoned the business by trading it for a farmstead in Loyal, some nine miles from the restaurant. His plan was to eventually hire a third party to operate the farmstead but move the family there to do so in the interim. That, too, failed. Undeterred, the family packed as much as they could into their vehicle, leaving behind furniture, equipment and numerous personal items, and went to live with Eva's parents on a farm eleven miles north of Chippewa Falls.[27] For Ralph, he had hit rock bottom.

For the next few years, Ralph, Eva and the boys lived on the Webb farm in Anson Township. It was here that both Robert, thirteen, and Harry, five, learned the value of hard work through a plethora of age-suitable chores around the property. Of course, it was the eldest son, Robert, who ended up completing a majority of the workload. Despite the work, the boys enjoyed their time on the farm. Free time was spent playing games, visiting friends or neighbors or gallivanting around the land. It was here that

Harry's third grade report card, circa 1927. *Author's collection.*

Harry celebrated his fifth birthday. The *Chippewa Herald-Telegram* reported that the young boy had "entertained a few friends…and was presented a cake with five birthday candles."[28]

Growing up on the farm also proved to be beneficial to Harry's academic success. In his two surviving Chippewa County Public School report cards, Harry earned high marks while attending the rural Anson schoolhouse in both first grade and second grade. As Harry advanced into the third grade, he had scored 90 percent or higher in deportment (95 percent), industry (95 percent), spelling and pronunciation (93 percent), reading (93 percent), writing (90 percent), arithmetic (90 percent) and language and grammar (90 percent). His teacher, Ms. Severa Sylvia Lemke, praised the young Harry by encouraging him to "keep on working as fine as you did" and to "always remember…responsibility." Above all else, Ms. Lemke saw something special and unique within Harry that made her predict the following: "Someday you'll be a great *man!*"[29]

By contrast, Harry's older brother didn't score as well in the core academic areas. Instead, he displayed a strong aptitude for farming and automobiles. As a teenager, Robert was a leading member of Anson Township's 4-H Club, an organization rooted in agricultural pursuits that emphasized "head, heart, hands, and health." The primary goal was for the club's members to "develop citizenship, leadership, responsibility, and life skills" through a variety of projects and activities.

DESPITE EACH BOY'S INDIVIDUAL pursuits and successes, the unexpected death of Eva's father had significantly altered the direction of the family. He had succumbed to heart failure several years earlier,[30] presumably induced when a horse pinned him against a wall in the stable, and his death had left the family in sorrow and financial uncertainty. In addition to running the farm, Ralph took on several odd jobs, including summer work at the nearby Wissota Sand and Gravel Company.[31] During one harvesting season, the hardworking Ralph even traveled to a neighboring state, where he engaged in the tedious and laborious task of husking corn in Iowa. By the late 1920s, it seemed that life on the Anson Township farm was also unsustainable.[32]

Just when it seemed things couldn't get worse for the Kramers, global economic forces led to the stock market crash on October 29, 1929. What followed was the "longest, deepest, and most widespread" economic depression of the twentieth century.[33]

On October 28, 1930, one day shy of the one-year anniversary of the crash, the Kramer family left the Webb farm in Anson and moved into a rental property in Chippewa Falls. Located on the far eastern side of the city's East Hill, at 21 Well Street, the older two-story home would become the family's sanctuary throughout the remaining years of the Great Depression. Moving into the new, semi-urban environs were Ralph, age forty-five; Eva, fifty; Robert, nineteen; Harry, ten; and Eva's mother, Ualia, seventy-four.[34]

AS THE PRIMARY EARNER for the family, Ralph's struggle for continuous employment only worsened through the Depression. Ralph hoped that a move to Chippewa Falls would increase his prospects. He had a short stint as a dry goods salesman with wholesale giant Butler Brothers Company, based in Minneapolis, Minnesota.[35] After that, he worked as a Phillips 66 gasoline agent, at 603 North Bridge Street,[36] and then for the Golden Rule Oil Company, located on the corner of River and Bridge Streets.[37] Ralph, Eva and Ualia also made use of their collective talents in the kitchen to cook lunches for area schoolchildren in partnership with the city's Rutledge Charity organization.[38] Ralph even dabbled as an author, distributing a thirty-one-page history pamphlet for the centennial celebration of Chippewa Falls.[39] Considering the economic challenges of the time, the family was holding their own as best as they could.

Complicating matters, Robert's decision to leave school early left Ralph and Eva deeply disappointed. In lieu of a diploma, Robert was eager to enter the workforce. As a tenacious worker, Robert initially found work as a field hand on the Albert Ford farm, only to leave to work as a laborer in the Civilian Conservation Corps (CCC). Finally, Robert found his niche as an auto mechanic, working at a shop in downtown Chippewa Falls. Supplementing this major life change was the news that nineteen-year-old Robert had been courting a young lady named Marie Grip.[40]

Nineteen-year-old Marie, daughter of Anton and Elsie Grip, was born into a family of Norwegian descent. The Grips owned and operated a sprawling farmstead located near the old Webb farm in Anson Township.[41]

The wedding of Robert and Marie Kramer, 1933. Thirteen-year-old Harry is standing second from left, wearing a white shirt and necktie. *Author's collection.*

Harry's family, circa 1938. *Standing, from left to right:* Harry's mother, Eva; his nephew, Carl; his father, Ralph; and nineteen-year-old Harry. *Sitting or kneeling, from left to right:* Harry's nephews Gerald and David and Harry's older brother, Robert. *Author's collection.*

While Robert could be shy and reserved, he had been drawn to Marie's sociable personality. He also found her intelligent, organized and beautiful. As someone raised in a devoutly Lutheran home, Marie was deeply religious and frowned on excessive dancing and alcohol consumption.[42]

Despite the couple's obvious magnetism, Marie's parents disliked the union from the beginning. Robert's modest economic means, lack of a high school diploma and lackluster interest in attending church may have played a role. Regardless, Robert and Marie united in marriage on September 6, 1933, and built their new home on a section of the Grips' farmstead.[43] Anton and Elsie's low opinion of Robert, however, would often percolate to the surface in the form of actions, opinions, comments and mannerisms and other gestures. In response, Robert largely kept his head down, as his unwavering devotion and love for Marie was always his primary focus. Within the next seven years, Robert and Marie would welcome four boys: Carl (1934), Gerald (1936), David (1938) and Earl (1940).[44]

Chapter 3

HARRY WELLINGTON KRAMER
OF CHIPPEWA FALLS

With Robert officially moved out of the house, Harry remained as the only child living at the 21 Well Street residence. Living in the city offered young Harry more opportunities in academics, religion, entertainment and friendships. Harry's public high school, for example, was only a twenty-minute walk away via city sidewalks. There, he maintained a recurrent honor roll status among the core academic subjects, as well as the manual trade school classes. In woodworking, it was Harry's perfectly crafted "flat top desk" that got the attention of the local newspaper.[45] Two years later, Harry and a classmate created a metal shop exhibit for the Northern Wisconsin State Fair. The submission included a display showing the "kinds of threads used in vises, cars, bolts, and machines," as well as a "taper to show how tapers are used for lathes."[46]

Downtown was also home to the Kramers' new church, where Harry spent a lot of time and developed numerous friends and acquaintances. Located on West Spring Street, in the lodge building owned by the Odd Fellows fraternal group, the Church of Christ, Scientist's version of Christianity promoted physical and mental healing through prayer and spiritual teachings. The family had made the conversion several years prior, and Harry found the faith exhilarating. Harry's devout religious observance garnered him much respect and adoration from his parents, especially his mother.[47]

For entertainment purposes, Chippewa Falls offered a variety of options that suited the teenage Harry's outdoor interests. He would swim in the millpond off Bridgewater Avenue, near Marshall Park. Other times, he liked to fish and hike along Duncan Creek, rated the best trout stream in

The Kramer family home at 21 Well Street, on the East Hill of Chippewa Falls. *Author's collection.*

the county. Most of the time, however, Harry could be found, either alone or accompanied by a friend or two, exploring the city's iconic Irvine Park, located two miles from the Kramer house. Harry explored the trails and cliffs, swam in Glen Loch Lake, ate picnic lunches, camped in a tent, took in public concerts and visited the zoo animals housed there.[48]

Above all else, the city provided ample opportunities for the teenage Harry to meet new friends and acquaintances. Through his time at Chippewa Falls High School, Harry became chummy with several of his classmates, including Loyal Lubach, Benjamin "Benny" Smith, Jack Larson and Earl White. Harry's two closest friends were Mortimer "Mort" Anderson and John "Jack" Selden. Mort was only two months older than Harry and lived a block away at 120 Division Street. The two spent so much time together around the neighborhood that Ralph and Eva affectionately referred to Mort as "their other boy."[49]

Jack, by contrast, was five and a half years younger than Harry and a distant relative from Eva's side of the family.[50] The Seldens lived in a two-story home on the city's west hill, at 315 West Elm Street. Jack and his family were also active in the Church of Christ, Scientist, where the two boys would see each other frequently. The Seldens viewed Harry as a positive influence on their young son, as he was level-headed and possessed a strong moral compass. Jack's younger sister Jean remembered Harry as "quiet, sweet, a bit

SEVENTH GRADE

Above: Fourteen-year-old Harry in the seventh grade, 1933. *Author's collection.*

Right: Harry's good friend Jack Selden and his younger sister Jean, undated. *Author's collection.*

Eighteen-year-old Harry as a graduating senior, 1938. *Author's collection.*

reserved, and just an overall good role model for Jack."[51]

Harry's high school reputation validated this description. Nicknamed "Ramsey," possibly after the mathematician Frank Ramsey, Harry was known as an old soul who largely kept to himself. Despite his prowess in academics and the trades, Harry showed little interest in extracurricular activities. Team sports, clubs, plays and dances were not Harry's preference. He was drawn to more individual and unstructured pursuits. When he declared to the yearbook staff that his favorite hobby was swimming, this led them to prophesize that one day he might become a "deep sea diver," combining his love of swimming with his desire for a career as a machinist. By contrast, his good friend Mort participated in sports and clubs and volunteered to co-organize the junior prom dance, a dance Harry did not attend.[52]

On Thursday, June 3, 1938, the graduating class of Chippewa Falls Senior High School gathered at Irvine Park for the annual class day picnic, where a short program was followed by a celebratory lunch. Of the 129 seniors, Harry ranked 14th in his class. His years of hard work and determination had paid off, as both family and school staff were convinced that Harry would achieve big things in life. Ralph and Eva hoped that his school career would springboard Harry into an economic prosperity that no one else in the family had yet attained.[53]

The next evening, on June 3, graduating students and their families filled the junior high school's auditorium to capacity. The commencement address was given by Dr. Jim Hill, president of the Superior State Teachers College. Dr. Hill challenged the graduates to never stop learning by "taking time to read articles and books on world and national problems." He warned against blindly accepting political and media propaganda and warned of the rise of communism and fascism around the world. "The greatest bulwark against these forces is American democracy," Hill proclaimed, "with the bulwark of democracy being serious reading and thinking being done by our citizens."[54]

Following Hill was an address made by valedictorian Ruth Larrabee. Her speech was followed by several musical numbers. Principal Howard M. Lyon praised the graduates for their work and accomplishments and concluded the ceremony by distributing diplomas. Harry Wellington Kramer was ready to take his own life's journey.[55]

As a graduation gift to their son, Ralph and Eva gave Harry a train ticket so he could visit relatives in Montana. For two months, Harry lived with George and Louise Simpson of Livingston. Louise had been the wife of Eva's brother Earl, who had died several years prior. She remarried but remained close to Earl's family. While out west, Harry indulged in all of the outdoor activities he had a passion for back home, but on a grander scale. He hiked high into area mountains, fished numerous streams and rivers and camped alone in remote locales. Most memorably, Harry spent two weeks exploring Yellowstone National Park. There he marveled at giant waterfalls, powerful geysers and different types of fauna and flora he had never seen. It was the farthest from home he had ever been, and he cherished the experience.[56]

Fresh off his return, Harry contemplated a career as a local machinist. With the Great Depression still making good-paying jobs scarce, Harry contemplated joining the military. The U.S. Navy, in particular, had fleets of ships that required machinists to work below their decks. The navy also provided free lodging, three meals a day and a guaranteed paycheck. Harry figured he could make money while also saving money. In addition, he could financially aid his father, mother and grandmother, if needed. Looming over all of this were the fond memories Harry kept from Montana. Enlisting in the navy would bring adventure.

In December 1939, Harry and his father visited the U.S. Navy's recruiting substation in downtown Chippewa Falls. Harry informed the two recruiters, P.J. Class and Fred A. Franz, that his reason for enlistment was to "learn a trade." With the rise of fascism and communism around the world, government leaders in the United States had been proactively trying to build up the country's peacetime military forces. Class and Franz both encouraged the twenty-year-old Harry to join, as the navy would satisfy all his life goals.

Despite their initial enthusiasm, the recruiters expressed two concerns regarding Harry's enlistment. First, ambiguities on Harry's birth certificate needed to be rectified. Second, Franz was concerned that Harry might not be able to pass the navy's basic dental requirements. He was born with a large occlusion in his mouth, where the upper incisor teeth overlap the lower ones, more commonly known as an "overbite." The navy avoided recruits with such abnormalities, as they could hinder a sailor's ability to verbally communicate or even eat his assigned military rations. Franz informed Harry that the physical would take place in Minneapolis and the final determination would be made there.

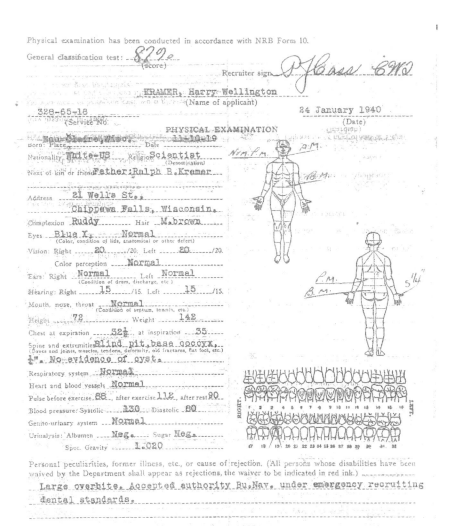

Harry's physical examination results, 1940. *National Archives.*

On the evening of Monday, January 22, 1940, Harry's parents, his grandmother Ualia and his brother, Robert, and sister-in-law, Marie, gathered at a Chippewa Falls train station to see Harry off to Minneapolis. If all went well with his physical examination, including a special dental waiver, Harry would immediately be transferred to Great Lakes, Illinois, for naval boot camp. Once Harry completed boot camp, the plan was for him to return to Chippewa Falls so the family could celebrate prior to his deployment. After a series of emotional goodbyes, Harry boarded his train and left for Minneapolis.

Unbeknownst to everyone at the train station that evening, it was the last time they would ever lay eyes on Harry.[57]

On his arrival to the U.S. Navy's recruiting station in Minneapolis, on January 24, Harry was given a physical by medical examiner and navy lieutenant C.D. Bell. Bell described Harry as standing 6'0" tall, weighing 142 pounds, having blue eyes and medium brown hair and displaying an overall ruddy, or reddish, complexion. Bell wrote that Harry had a resting pulse of 88 and a blood pressure of 120/80 and he possessed normal hearing and vision. Concluding that Harry had no major or obvious health concerns, he went on to document all the distinguishable features, or personal markers, unique to Harry on a body diagram.

Close-up of Harry, showing detailed facial characteristics, 1940. *Author's collection.*

On his anterior side, or front, Harry had one pinhead mole on the left side of his neck, as well a few on the right side. A small birthmark was noted on his abdomen, just to the right of center. On his posterior side, a pinhead mole was noted in the middle of his back, on his left side. A quarter-inch scar was highlighted on the top of his right hand, near the webbing where his thumb met the index finger. Lastly, Harry had a sacral pit, or dimple, at the base of his lower back, supplemented by a birthmark just to the left.[58]

Bell also completed a dental chart, which revealed that Harry was missing one of his permanent adult teeth, a first molar on the bottom right side of his jaw. As for Harry's large overbite, Bell confessed that the deficiency would have normally disqualified him from service. But due to the navy's immediate need for more enlisted men, numerous candidates were being exempted if the medical concern was low risk. Ultimately, Harry was "accepted" under the authority of the Bureau of Navigation's "emergency recruiting dental standards."[59] With the issue settled, Harry was now heading to boot camp. On January 27, the *Eau Claire Leader-Telegram* announced that two area men had officially enlisted in the navy and would eventually be stationed aboard ships within the fleet: twenty-year-old Harry Wellington Kramer of Chippewa Falls and twenty-two-year-old Frank Edward Nicoles of Eau Claire. While it's unclear if the two ever encountered each other in person, this would not be the last time their names were referenced alongside each other.[60]

PART II
Letters from Harry

Chapter 1

1940: FROM NAVAL BOOT CAMP
TO THE USS *CALIFORNIA*

Letter No. 1: Harry Kramer to his friend Jack Selden
February 11, 1940
From: U.S. Naval Training Station, Great Lakes, IL
To: Chippewa Falls, WI

On Thursday, January 25, less than twenty-four hours after taking the U.S. Navy's Oath of Allegiance in Minneapolis, Harry disembarked his train near the entrance to the United States Naval Training Station in Great Lakes, Illinois. It was situated on the southwestern shores of Lake Michigan, its geographic location near equally set between the urban centers of Milwaukee, Wisconsin, and Chicago, Illinois. Having already served the nation's military needs during the First World War, the Great Lakes facility expected to play an even larger role if the nation was to go to war against either Japan or Germany.[61]

With some three hundred miles of distance between him and his friend Jack, Harry enjoyed the first days of boot camp and eagerly gave Jack a full report. As a new arrival, Harry was assigned to "Incoming Detention Camp," or Camp Barry, a collection of brick buildings in the southwestern corner of the naval station. There, arrivals received their medical exams, inoculations, haircuts, uniforms and a litany of drills and exercises aimed at forging a high level of naval discipline in the ranks. During peacetime, a newbie would spend twenty-one days here. "Detention Camp," as Harry

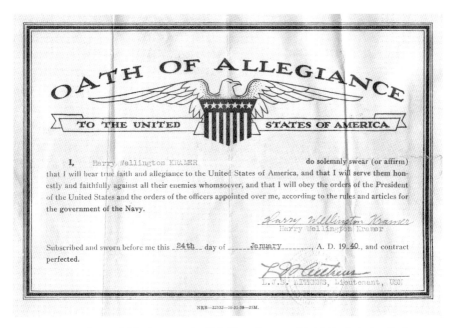

Harry's signed Oath of Allegiance to the U.S. Navy, January 24, 1940. *Author's collection.*

called it, was the navy's abrupt way of beginning the process of determining who would be a good fit and who wouldn't. Primarily, the camp's function was to segregate the arrivals, as a means to keep communicable diseases away from the others on base.[62]

If Harry felt any misgivings about his decision to join the navy, he didn't reveal anything in this first letter home. As a young man whose formative years had been shaped by the economic challenges of the Great Depression, Harry relished this opportunity. He expressed gratefulness and excitement to be eating the food served to him in the mess hall.[63]

> *Dear Jack,*
>
> *Last Wednesday, the company clerk handed me the envelope containing your mother's letter and I was sure pleased. I am sorry I was not more prompt in writing. The first week was one of confusion and haste…..No time even to go to the canteen for stationery.*
>
> *I suppose since I left, you have been wondering what has been going on around here. When we arrived they gave us another physical exam. Next, the clothes were issued and arranged in special order so our names could be quickly stenciled. I got here on a Thursday morning and that night we had*

our clothes, mattress, blankets, etc. and shown to our barracks. At the time we came, all the main brick buildings were filled so we had to use these wooden barracks. Although they were comfortable it is half a mile to the mess hall. Marching to and from meals takes up a lot of time but nobody seems to mind because we are always good and hungry.

The food is very good and quite a variety. We always form a line with a large rectangular tin plate and it is filled with five or six different kinds of food. If anyone wants more he lines up a second time. This week they gave us pie every noon. On Sundays we have chicken and ice cream or pie for dessert. I still miss good old home made buns though.

We worked nearly all day on our clothes for inspection. Saturday is always inspection day and our sea bags have to be in perfect order. There is quite a trick to rolling clothes. It is a lot of fun after a little practice. We have four suits of whites, three suits of blues, four towels, four sets of underwear, one sweater, four hats, three pairs of shoes, and a lot of smaller things…handkerchiefs, soap, etc.

Next Thursday will be the end of our three weeks in detention camp.… We can move over to the other side called "Paradise." There we will start sleeping in hammocks which are eight feet off the floor and will be able to go swimming, use the library, and maybe have it a little easier all around. Perhaps, I'll get more time to write.

Harry's initial boot camp home, Camp Barry (a.k.a. Incoming Detention Camp), circa 1940. *Author's collection.*

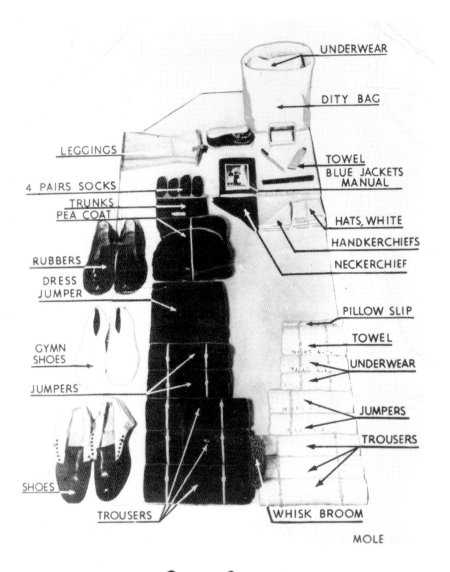

UNDERWEAR

DITY BAG

LEGGINGS

TOWEL
BLUE JACKETS
MANUAL

4 PAIRS SOCKS

TRUNKS
PEA COAT

HATS, WHITE

HANDKERCHIEFS

RUBBERS

NECKERCHIEF

DRESS
JUMPER

PILLOW SLIP

TOWEL

GYMN
SHOES

UNDERWEAR

JUMPERS

JUMPERS

TROUSERS

SHOES

TROUSERS

WHISK BROOM

MOLE

Bag Lay-out
U. S. NAVAL TRAINING CENTER
GREAT LAKES, ILLINOIS

Boot camp diagram for sea bag inspections, circa 1940. *Author's collection.*

*The night watch just stepped in and said "Lights out in ten minutes" so it
means I'll have to end this right away. Tell your mother, father, grandmother
[Mrs. Gailey] and sister Jean "Hello" and that I miss seeing them. It
won't be long before I can come back on boot leave.*
    Your pal,
    Harry

Letter No. 2: Harry Kramer to his friend Jack Selden
February 18, 1940
From: U.S. Naval Training Station, Great Lakes, IL
To: Chippewa Falls, WI

Within the twenty-four days since Harry had arrived at Great Lakes Naval
Training Station, relations between the United States and Japan had
deteriorated. A commercial pact between the two nations signed in 1911
had expired in late January. Both Congress and President Franklin Roosevelt
contemplated economic embargoes against the militaristic empire. Japan's
1937 invasion of China had caused bipartisan consternation, which, at
the time, led to a ban on weapon transports to Japan. With the expiration
of the pact, Roosevelt mulled an additional ban on the exportation of all
natural resources, as well as a general duty increase on all Japanese imports
to the United States.[64]

    In Washington, D.C., Roosevelt's call for Congress to pass $1.3 billion
in naval funding had been pared back to just under $1 billion by a House
committee. The most significant item removed was funding to transform
the Pacific Island of Guam into a "naval lookout post" by building
fortifications and making significant harbor improvements. Located some
1,500 miles away from Tokyo, Guam was 1,800 miles closer to Japan than
Pearl Harbor was. Roosevelt viewed the fortification of Guam as a major
check against future Japanese aggression. Detractors felt this would only
serve to increase tensions between the two nations and thus jettisoned the
Guam proposal from the bill.[65]

    Other stories covered by the *Chippewa Herald-Telegram* included fascist Italy
doubling the size of its air force,[66] the execution of two Americans by the
Nazis in the Wawer Massacre in Poland[67] and President Roosevelt sending
his undersecretary of state to Europe to meet with representatives of other
neutral nations regarding the ongoing conflicts.[68]

At the Great Lakes Naval Training Station, Harry had made it through the initial "Detention Camp" and was eager to move on to "Paradise Camp." Unfortunately, a mumps outbreak lengthened his company's stay. In addition to bayonet and firearm drills, Harry wrote about mandatory church attendance, wearing his blue navy dress uniform and eating a lot of good food.[69]

Dear Jack,

Our company just returned from chow and we have nothing to do, which is very unusual....Last night I had watch from 2 to 4 AM so it feels good to have today to myself. On Sundays we can sleep till 6:00 but this morning we got up at 5:00. I wish you could be in the mess hall and see how fast the food disappears. For breakfast I had scrambled eggs, four slices of bread, fried potatoes, fifteen pieces of bacon and an orange. Because we were at early chow we could not go for seconds or I would have been back for more. Someone just told me they used 110 dozen eggs for breakfast this morning which does not include "Paradise Camp." About three times a week they give us fruit salad for dessert. Golly it is delicious. It is made of oranges, apples, pieces of grapefruit, raisins, and coconut. There is usually quite a bit of this left....So I took my soup bowl up and had that filled. Today, being Sunday, we should have chicken and ice cream for dinner.

The normal period in detention camp is three weeks and I should be writing this letter from the other side, called "Paradise." Well, last Thursday, the day we were to move, we got packed up and ready when orders came that both Company 6 and 7 were under quarantine for mumps. We were all disappointed...but later learned that if no new cases broke out they would let us go. Company 6 has had two or three cases.... But we have not. So we may leave tomorrow.

It is required that we go to church every Sunday, but not today because of quarantine. We always wear dress blues with a neckerchief and a flat hat. Easter Sunday, the last Sunday before coming home we will wear dress whites for the first time. We are all wondering how we will sleep in a hammock. One boy fell out four times during the first night. Golly some fun!

We were issued bayonets and practiced placing them on our guns. Nearly every day we have been working on a series of rifle and arm exercises. When we move to "Paradise" each company is in competition with each other....The best record in exercises, athletics, and cleanliness wins what is known as the "Rooster" for that week and get a 36 hour leave. Naturally, every company watches out for themselves.

Is there anything happening at home? How much have you finished on your radio cabinet? I miss going up to school and working in the shops. I spoke to Mother about giving you my white t-shirt for skating so if you ever go up to the house be sure and get it. It might as well be used by someone. How has the weather been for skating? We have had only a few really cold days but it is rather chilly when the sun is not out.

I can't remember all I wrote to you last time, so please overlook anything I repeated. Give my regards to all the family.

Your pal,

Harry

———

Letter No. 3: Harry Kramer to his friend Jack Selden
March 3, 1940
From: U.S. Naval Training Station, Great Lakes, IL
To: Chippewa Falls, WI

Midway through Harry's naval boot camp, the nation's newspapers reported on the foreign meetings of the undersecretary of state, Sumner Welles. Sent by Roosevelt on a fact-finding mission to ascertain the war situation, Welles first traveled to Rome to meet with fascist leader Benito Mussolini. Despite their "neutral position" on the war between Britain, France and Germany, Italy seemed close to forming an alliance with Adolf Hitler's Germany. During this visit, however, Sumner told the press he was not releasing any information but that his meeting with Mussolini had been "long and cordial."[70]

The next day, Welles traveled to Berlin and met with Hitler. After the meeting, the press reported that "Hitler Demands Peace on His Own Terms." Hitler argued for a "Monroe Doctrine for Germany" and for all ancestral and war-lost lands to be returned to his people. He also demanded that Great Britain relinquish military control of "Gibraltar, the Suez Canal, and other strategic points of interest," as Hitler sought to access those shipping lanes. Unsurprisingly, Welles reported to Roosevelt that Hitler was not ready for peace and that "Germany is set to continue their present setup."[71]

Other related stories published prominently in the *Chippewa Herald-Telegram* were that Germany had moved large amounts of troops to the Luxembourg border,[72] air and sea warfare had renewed between Britain and Germany[73] and Roosevelt made a surprise inspection trip to the Panama Canal Zone in Central America.[74]

As global politics intensified, Harry learned that he would not be receiving the customary twelve-day boot leave after graduation. Instead, he would travel directly to Long Beach, California, and be assigned to a naval vessel in time for its spring maneuvers. With just twenty-four days left, Harry used his free time to explore the non-quarantined areas of the base, including a popular reading, writing and recreational space called "Hostess House."

In a tender and nostalgic moment, Harry mentioned the cookies and "Cracker Jacks" that Jessie Selden (Jack's mother) had mailed him. The molasses-flavored, caramel-coated popcorn and peanut treat utilized a sailor named Jack, along with his dog Bingo, as mascots.[75] Subsequently, navy uniforms were nicknamed "cracker jacks." Mrs. Selden's reference was not lost on Harry, and he appreciated both the gesture and the treat.

One peculiar aspect of Harry's third letter is that it abruptly ends mid-sentence. It's possible that an additional page or pages were misplaced or lost. However, the partial sentence at the end begins with the words "when our company commander." More than likely, Harry's letter was censored by an officer.[76] This assigned individual would make sure no sensitive information left base and was empowered to remove pages, cut out small or large sections and confiscate or simply discard the letter. This could all be done with or without notification to the sender.[77]

> *Dear Jack,*
>
> *It is gray and dreary outside…with rain coming down now and then. I am now in "Paradise" and like it fine although we do not have much more time off than in Camp Barry. Things are much more convenient over here and there is a greater variety of things to do. The mess hall is now right out the back door. The scrub room is in the basement and that is certainly handy.*
>
> *We moved over a week ago which made us a week late on account of the quarantine. There have been no new mumps cases so I guess everything is alright with the other company. They had it pretty bad before.*
>
> *There is a swell building just across the creek called the Hostess House, where the boys can go to read, write, play games such as checkers, cards, etc. and use the canteen or buy ice cream. However, they charge quite a bit. Those swell chocolate Sundaes we had in Eau Claire* [Wisconsin] *that cost a dime would be twice the amount here.*

Hostess House, a popular recreational center in "Paradise Camp," circa 1940. *Author's collection.*

Tomorrow, we will go to the rifle range for the first time. 22's are used and when shooting you lay down on a mat. We have been having a competitive drill in marching and semaphore signaling. We are also learning to tie knots. Right now we are busy studying for a seaman's test. We are to know all the parts of an oar, a sailboat, a sail, an anchor, etc.

Tell your mother thanks a million for the lovely cookies and Cracker Jacks. Gosh, that home cooking tastes swell. I guess there are other good cooks baking things for us sailors because the packages seem to arrive daily. I don't blame the boys for smiling when they get a box because you don't know how good your mothers' cooking is until you leave.

*I told Mother I would surely eat a lot when I came home on my 12-day boot leave after graduating on the 27*th* of March. But, I have surprising news. I am not going to get boot leave at all. On the 30*th*, I will leave for California and will be out to sea for spring fleet maneuvers. I will get a chance to go to Hawaii. How's that for a change in orders? It happened last Friday when our company commander...*

[The rest of the letter is missing.]

Letter No. 4: Harry Kramer to his friend Jack Selden
March 14, 1940
From: U.S. Naval Training Station, Great Lakes, IL
To: Chippewa Falls, WI

March saw the situation in Europe become more arduous, as neutral Italy was angered when Great Britain seized five of its freighters sailing toward Germany. Each was filled with precious coal Hitler needed to maintain his war machine. Mussolini demanded passage, citing his nation's neutrality. Ultimately, the British let the ships pass but directed that all future coal shipments be transported via overland routes.[78]

Not all was bad news for Britain, as it successfully evacuated the newly constructed RMS *Queen Elizabeth* when the world's largest passenger liner arrived safely in New York. It had been "painted a drab gray" to camouflage it from German air bombings and secretly moved at night.[79] Germany, meanwhile, celebrated its own version of Memorial Day. Hitler gave an "On-to-Victory" speech, reaffirming his commitment to defeating Great Britain and France.[80]

Back at the Great Lakes Naval Training Center, Harry learned that his graduation and ship date had been advanced by a week. Leaving on March 23, instead of the thirtieth, he would be transported by a special troop train to California and then assigned to a ship. When asked if he had a preference, Harry wrote, "Battleship."

One day at camp, while observing a marching group of recent graduates, Harry recognized a familiar face. Earl R. White had graduated Chippewa Falls High School with Harry in 1938 and enlisted just two weeks prior to Harry. Both men had a knack for working with their hands and were similarly drawn to careers working with ship engines. Unlike Harry, however, Earl got to keep his boot leave after graduation and promptly returned home to Chippewa Falls. Earl, too, would soon report to California, as he had been assigned to the battleship USS *Oklahoma*.[81]

Dear Jack,

   Today has been one of rush and confusion trying to get everything straightened out for inspection but as it is evening now I'll have till bedtime to write a few lines. This morning we listened to an instructor tell us of all the details of a five-inch gun which is installed in the armory. Half of our final exams will contain questions on guns and ammunition and today was the first we learned about the larger ones.

Harry (shown with an *X* beneath his feet) standing with his company in the main drill hall at the U.S. Naval Training Station in Great Lakes, Illinois, March 17, 1940. *Author's collection.*

We do not have much marching to do anymore…only when there is a dress parade for the graduating companies. Yesterday we watched companies 2 and 3 go through the armory for the last time. Earl White stood just in front of me in company 2.

I enjoyed the article you sent….Thanks a lot. I would buy more things to read and study such as Sentinels and Journals but it is just a short while until I leave for the coast and with the extra clothing allowance we will receive there will not be any room to pack anything more. Every day we are in this station we have to wear leggings but now when we leave for California they do not have to be worn. However, we will still pack them up with the other clothes and take them along.

I told you, I believe, in my last letter that I was to leave for the coast on the 30th of March, but since then orders came in setting the date a week earlier on Saturday, March 23rd. Well, that is just a few days away and we are trying to finish things up in a hurry. There will be four companies, using two special trains. The different orders which our commander receives have been changed so often that we don't know what to expect. They might get an idea to send us 323 men even sooner for all I know. Our commander had us write down after our names what type of ship we preferred. I put down a battleship.

It is now 9 o'clock or in navy time the same as 2100 or two bells. That means I'll have to begin folding up my clothes and make up my hammock. Best wishes for all.

Your pal,
Harry

Letter No. 5: Harry Kramer to his friend Jack Selden
March 25, 1940
From: Aboard a Troop Train near Deming, NM
To: Chippewa Falls, WI

The last few weeks of March ushered in significant changes to the war landscape in Europe. Hitler and Mussolini held a secret in-person meeting on March 18.[82] At the meeting, Hitler pressured Mussolini to immediately join the war. Caving to Hitler's pressure, Mussolini agreed to end Italy's neutrality at an opportune moment. The two leaders also indicated that they would try to lure the Soviet Union onto their side, as they continued to wage war against the British and French.[83]

News accounts out of Japan, meanwhile, reported that Prime Minister Mitsumasa Yonai and Admiral Zengo Yoshida had assured the press that "Japan's Navy is 'ready to meet any situation' resulting from the current expansion of the United States Navy." Both men, however, remained optimistic that relations with the United States could still be improved.[84]

It was against this backdrop that Harry graduated from naval boot camp. Harry wrote this letter while riding aboard a special troop train transporting hundreds of sailors from Great Lakes to Long Beach. He seemed to savor the ride, as he commented on the distinctive countryside that differed so greatly from Wisconsin. He also revealed that his request to serve on a battleship had been granted, as the USS *California* was to be his new home. To share the excitement of the news, Harry purchased a postcard of the ship and mailed it to his parents. Harry had gone from a green naval enlistee to a fully graduated apprentice seaman.[85]

Dear Jack,

I am sitting in car number 2 of a fifteen car train, looking out at the desert with hundreds of cacti and mountains beyond. We are nearing Deming, New Mexico and the time is 8:30 AM. Last Saturday, our train left Great Lakes at 4:00 PM with 333 sailors. Number 1 train left with 323 men, so a total of 656 sailors will arrive in California on Tuesday. This is the biggest draft since the war. So far we have passed through Illinois, Missouri, Kansas, Oklahoma, Texas, and New Mexico...soon to enter Arizona. Yesterday, while going through Kansas, I did not enjoy the scenery half as much...as it was flat as a sheet of glass and did not have a tree on it. Although it is dry desert country down here...it is much more interesting. The conductor told us the temperature reached 100 degrees yesterday. I can hardly realize that I am not coming to Livingston, Montana, for that was where I saw mountains for the first time.

We are now in Arizona. Our next stop may be at Tucson but the train usually stays only five or ten minutes at each station.

The meals are a swell change from the usual things back at the training station. Something we all enjoy is plenty of butter. About every

Aerial view of the USS *California* battleship, circa 1940. *U.S. Navy.*

other meal they give us ice cream. There is one thing I'd like though and that is pancakes.

I sent some more pictures home which I bought at Great Lakes. One of them is a large view of the ship I am to be on, the USS California. I wanted to send one to you but they were sold out. However, if you go up to the house sometime, Mother will show you.

Pardon the scribbling but it's hard to write while the train is swaying from side to side.

Your pal,

Harry

———

Letter No. 6: Harry Kramer to Mrs. Jessie Selden (Mother of Jack Selden)
March 25, 1940
From: Aboard a Troop Train in Eastern Arizona
To: Chippewa Falls, WI

After completing his letter to Jack, Harry decided to write to Jessie Selden, Jack's mom. To her, Harry revealed his religious side, as he referenced the two most important books in the faith of the Church of Christ, Scientist. First is the Holy Bible, and second is *Science and Health with Key to the Scriptures*. He could comfortably discuss religion with Mrs. Selden, as the Seldens also belonged to the First Church of Christ, Scientist, in Chippewa Falls. Written by Church of Christ, Scientist founder Mary Baker Eddy in 1875, *Science and Health* details the church's theology and methods for self-healing, which derive from the following lines:

> *God is All-in all;*
> *God is good;*
> *God is Mind, and God is infinite; hence all is Mind.*

Mary Baker Eddy created the church to restore a more organic Christianity that she felt had been lost over time. One of the church's more well-known, yet controversial, beliefs was that human sickness was a product of personal belief, not a property of matter. Eddy taught that praying to God, from this standpoint, could remove the belief of sickness and thus deliver healing. Her book is filled with various testimonials of healing, from maladies such as asthma and addiction to rheumatism and tumors.[86]

This is also the first time Harry acknowledged having a "touch of homesickness." As a coping mechanism, Harry quoted another of Eddy's books, *Miscellaneous Writings, 1833–1896*, as proof that his faith had helped him manage. Harry knew, as he gazed at the cacti whizzing by him through the train window, that he might not get the chance to go home anytime soon.[87]

Dear Mrs. Selden,

I have always enjoyed your letters but have neglected to send one in return.

We have just passed into Arizona and it is getting very hot. By noon it will be at least 95 degrees and [we] *will change into white hats and remove our jerseys. I just looked out the window and saw an acre of pretty orange Indian flowers, growing among the cacti and sagebrush. This would be a nice place to use a camera.*

Last week, Mother sent a small Bible that I used at home, and it goes well with the Science & Health books. On this trip there is plenty of time for reading and…at night too, while things are quiet and I am lying in my berth I read and know that although we may go hundreds of miles in any direction we cannot be without the ever operative laws of divine science and the omnipotence of God. The words which Miss Thomas read to me from "Miscellaneous Writings," page 150 I believe, helped me overcome a touch of homesickness—"Space is no separator of hearts." Whenever I can get time off, I want to go to the reading rooms on the coast.

I would have enjoyed seeing you folks….But they wanted us on that trip to the islands and so all of us had to go without vacation. I don't know when we can come home, this summer I hope.

We are now passing over a real desert…not even a weed on its flat sandy surface. In the distance is a mirage of a big lake….Hard to believe that there is not a drop of water out there.

I'm sending the handkerchief as a little souvenir…made from the fiber of a cactus plant.

Please give my regards to Mrs. Gailey, Ralph, and Jean.

Best wishes and love,

Harry

Letter No. 7: Harry Kramer to his mother, Eva Kramer
April 13, 1940
From: USS California
To: Chippewa Falls, WI

During the last week of March, Hitler accused the United States of planning to enter the war on behalf of Great Britain and France. He claimed to have seized secret documents from a Polish official's office in Berlin that outlined the plan.[88] In response, Roosevelt dismissed his claims and remarked, "Propaganda from abroad should be taken with several grains of salt." Days later, Hitler's army took over Denmark and invaded Norway.[89]

In London, negative public opinion led to a shake-up of Prime Minister Neville Chamberlain's cabinet. The "hard-hitting Winston Churchill" was promoted to lead the "British War Setup."[90] Over in China, the Japanese announced the creation of a new "central government" to rule over the Chinese people living in their conquered areas.[91]

As Harry's westward train arrived in Los Angeles County on March 26, 1940, he had little time to spare. He was expected to report to his battleship later in the day. Harry arrived on time, boarded his ship and began the adventure of a navy sailor.

The USS *California* was one of two Tennessee-class battleships ordered by the U.S. Navy in 1915. Harry was only ten days old when the new ship was launched from Vallejo, California, on November 20, 1919. Nicknamed "the Prune Barge," after one of California's largest fruit exports, the battleship's maximums were 624 feet long and 97 feet wide. The vessel's top speed was 21 knots (24 miles per hour), and it was designed with a cruising range of 9,200 miles. *California* was armed with a main battery of twelve 14-inch guns (50 caliber), which were arranged in four 3-gun turrets, placed as two super firing pairs on both the forward and aft sides of the ship. The secondary battery included fourteen 50-inch guns (51 caliber), mounted individually in casemates in the superstructure. Supplementing these were two 21-inch torpedo tubes, mounted in the hull on each of the ship's broadsides.[92]

During his time at boot camp, Harry had communicated with his parents via telephone. Now, living on the move far from home, long-distance phone calls were not a practical option. In his first letter written to his mother, Harry revealed his natural wonder and excitement for life before him as a sailor on the earth's largest ocean. So many things were new to him, including

Harry in his blue U.S. Navy uniform, circa 1940. *Author's collection.*

the strong and unimpeded ocean winds, the gigantic waves and the nauseating feeling of seasickness.

Harry also revealed where his battle station was aboard the ship. During an emergency, an announcement of "general quarters" indicated that every man needed to report to their assigned battle station. Harry's was located belowdecks, in the lower handling room of gun turret—or barbette—number two. Here he would be part of a human chain whose mission was to pass bags of gunpowder from one room to another, which ultimately were used to shoot projectiles from the ship's massive guns.

Above all else, Harry joyfully conveyed the awe-inspiring experience of existing on a tropical island in the middle of the Pacific Ocean. His first stop was Lahaina, on the island of Maui. Lahaina was situated some ninety-one miles southeast of Pearl Harbor, and the navy used it as an alternative anchorage spot for its Pacific Fleet. Lahaina—meaning "cruel sun" in Hawaiian—is known for its warm, dry climate, seeing less than thirteen inches of rain per year.[93] During his free time, in a district of just 8,291 residents,[94] Harry swam, lay in the surf, explored for coral and tasted fresh sugarcane straight from the field.[95]

Dear Mother,

You and dad write such interesting letters. Well, I am finally in the Hawaiian Islands. I'll never forget the morning we left California. Of course, I had never had the feeling of the ship in motion….At first it was hard to walk around. The second day I felt a touch of seasickness….Since then I love the roll and pitch of the ship in heavy seas. Anytime I got off from work or it wasn't raining I would stand up on the boat deck and watch the waves pour down on the deck until it was four or five inches deep. By the time this run over the sides another would come.

All the way across, the ship was engaged in war maneuvers and… called to general quarters, by the loudspeakers. We hurry to our battle stations and prepare for action. My station is in the lower handling room of gun turret number 2. I help hand bags of powder to another room. It was just practice…so we just sat down or slept until they called us topside. I read a couple of western books. Because of these conditions the ship was usually darkened at sunset every night and there were no movies, etc. We are offshore only a few hundred yards from Lahaina. It is beautiful here. The mountains rise in the background and their lower slopes are covered with plantations of green growth, usually sugar cane. The island is lightly populated…one main street, with a mill, and a few other buildings scattered. This place is conveniently located and was formerly the capital until moved to Hawaii. There are dozens of other ships around at night…pretty sight to see them lit up. Last night I took my mattress…on the forecastle (folk-sill) beneath the stars. I had a wonderful night's rest because it was so cool.

I went to my first swimming party and boy did I have fun. I left the ship, along with sixty other boys, in a big motor launch and taken a half-mile up the beach. The boat anchored half a block offshore and we had to swim in. This was the first time I had been on the island… to explore. First, I went near a cliff and sought coral. It is hard as rock and forms in pretty floral patterns. Another boy and I went inland and ate sugar cane. It is swell…awfully sweet. The rest of the time I played in the surf, sitting in front of a wave and letting it carry me yards up on the sand beach. Oh how I'd like to stay here for a while.…We arrive in Pearl Harbor in two weeks. You see we are going out to sea.…That means I won't be able to write until the end of the month. Ouch! I just rubbed my sunburn.

When we come back from this cruise…will go to the Bremerton Yards in Washington for three months. That means I might get leave, wouldn't that be swell. I noticed on the bulletin board that a round trip train ticket from California to St. Paul, Minnesota is $53. I don't know if I'll have a chance to save that much.

I enjoyed the letter from Great Aunt Minnie and am looking forward to seeing her and the rest. Our ship will be at San Pedro four or five days before going to Washington, but I don't know if I'll be able to get off long enough to go over to La Jolla (CA). I'll write again as soon as I get to Hawaii.

Lovingly,
Harry

Letter No. 8: Harry Kramer to his mother, Eva Kramer
May 5, 1940
From: Pearl Harbor, Honolulu, HI
To: Chippewa Falls, WI

One week after Hitler celebrated his fifty-first birthday, the German leader confirmed the obvious, that his country was indeed at war with Norway.[96] In response to the expanded conflict, Roosevelt signed an executive order reaffirming the United States' position of neutrality.[97] This action was in lockstep with the isolationist views held by a majority of Americans at the time. Speaking to the governing board of the Pan American Union in Washington, D.C., the president said that leaders from the twenty-one North American and Latin American countries were "wishing to live in peace" but urged that they should "prepare to meet force, with force, if needed."[98]

In Hawaii, the USS *California* arrived at its berthing site at Naval Station Pearl Harbor. Located some ten miles west of the city of Honolulu, on the Hawaiian island of Oahu, Pearl Harbor had been an official naval facility since 1908. In the 1930s, major additions and upgrades made Pearl Harbor one of the navy's preeminent facilities. Unlike nearby Lahaina, Pearl Harbor had the accommodations to berth an entire fleet, including "drydocks, supply warehouses, barracks, machine shops, training equipment, and offices." In addition, Pearl Harbor had room for a warship's "fleet train," which included all of the "auxiliary service vessels" that provide all of the "food, fuel, ammunition, and maintenance service" needed for battle.[99]

Under orders from President Roosevelt, the *California*, along with a bulk of the U.S. Pacific Fleet, was sent to Pearl Harbor to serve as a symbolic deterrent against further Japanese aggression. In the meantime, the sailors got a heavy dose of naval routine aboard ship and a tropical "liberty," or free time, of forty-eight consecutive hours per week.[100]

Harry wasted little time during his liberty, as he eagerly sought to see and experience all that Oahu had to offer. This included swimming at Waikiki Beach, visiting the Royal Hawaiian Hotel, seeing the Royal Palace and soaking in the view at the Nuuanu Pali Lookout. The midwestern Harry couldn't help but marvel at the high prices of food and souvenirs and commented on how tasty the Hawaiian-grown pineapples were, compared to the stuff he never liked back home.[101]

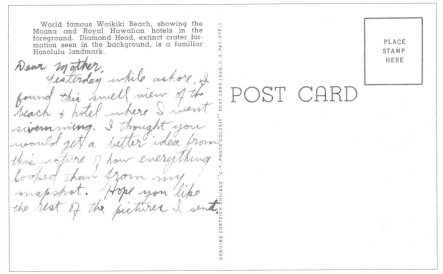

Top: Postcard featuring the Royal Hawaiian Hotel, Waikiki Beach and Diamondhead Crater in Honolulu, Hawaii, 1940. *Author's collection.*

Bottom: Reverse of postcard featuring a message Harry wrote to his mother, 1940. *Author's collection.*

Dear Mother,

There are so many things to say…about Hawaii. I have been going on a lot of trips about the island of Oahu. It sometimes seems like a dream. We are granted plenty of liberty so it is easy to get around and see things. Your letter came.…Tell Grandma Ualia and Dad "thanks a million" for theirs too. As grandma Ualia says, "I am always looking for mail" and notice the pleasure of the other boys when they get some too. On April 25ᵗʰ, when we came to the harbor, I went up on the boat deck that night to witness a searchlight display. I had never seen one before. Being surrounded by other ships, we could see all the beautiful designs in the sky. Each ship operates its battery from one side to the other, dozens of beams shooting up on the clouds all move at the same instant. I guess everyone in Honolulu stayed out to watch. It was so pretty.

It was hard to go to sleep that night, wondering what it would be like when we docked the next morning. When I got up it was pretty foggy from a rainstorm during the night. However as the ship approached the island and proceeded up the narrow river, it cleared and all the beautiful palms, flowers, and other growth came into view. Our ship got squared away at its dock and we spent the rest of the morning rigging awnings, fixing ropes, etc. I noticed right away what a wonderful climate they have. The temperature varies but a few degrees year around. I got liberty the first day and I hurried to get off. Liberty starts at 10:00 AM and ends at 7:00 PM which gives one quite a few hours. The harbor is six miles from Honolulu, so you have to get a taxi. I can hardly tell of the wonderful time I had that first day. Honolulu is made up of modern stores, office buildings, etc. and I walked all over just looking. The nicer places are surrounded by giant palms and hedges with big flower bushes scattered between. Most have signs reading "Welcome Navy" and they have their windows stuffed with souvenirs. A lot of the things are high.…They know the sailors would all be shopping. I guess it does cost more to live here because so many of the articles need to be shipped in…like eggs, butter, milk, etc. I saw a sign…which read "Butter 38 Cents."

The navy has two big YMCAs. One near the harbor and another in Honolulu. They are always packed with men of the fleet. I've been to both several times.

Although I had good times in Honolulu, the trips I took around the island were even more interesting. Last Tuesday four other boys and I hired a taxi and had a wonderful time sightseeing, taking pictures, etc. The driver was part Hawaiian and very nice. He took us to some places that other sailors did not see. We started from downtown and were shown the building that used to be the Royal Palace. It is now used by the governor, but retains the original throne room used by the former King and Queen. The next great place of interest was the "Pali." This spot is far above the city on a mountain and is famous because there one of the Kings of the island was supposed to have trapped his enemies on top of this cliff, and drove them over the edge of it (some 1,200 feet below). We got out and took pictures. It is one of the most beautiful places on the island if one wants a commanding view of the harbor, distant islands, ships, etc. Many visit this spot to witness the effect of a continuous strong wind, which blows up the roadway along the wall of the mountain. It can be calm anywhere else but at this place the wind is so strong it is hard to stand on your feet. During a windy day it has been known to stop cars. I am sending some pictures....You can see that we are leaning against the wind to stand and our clothes are whipping about us as if in a hurricane. They are bulky so I will send them by regular mail.

The rest of our trip was along the seashore....It is sure a wonderful place. On our way back to Honolulu...I saw some of the beautiful homes with different kinds of big trees and lattice work. The driver showed us where Shirley Temple, Sonia Hening [sic], etc. lived. The most beautiful building of all is the "Royal Hawaiian Hotel," outside the main part of town on the seashore. The grounds and its tropical foliage indicates a lot of work...no wonder it is well known. Dorothy Lamour and Bette Davis of the movies were there last week....Some of the men saw them at the beach.

Oh yes, I went swimming at the famous "Waikīkī Beach," located almost in front of the Hotel...which stretches for half a mile. I bought a new swimming suit the other day. They sell a $4.00 well-known brand of suit for $2.50. I got a blue one which I thought was nice and bright but when I arrived at the beach my eyes were nearly blinded by such gaudy colors. They are wearing flashy Hawaiian prints....Each one tries to outdo the other. I laid in the sand for a while just taking it all in. Boy oh boy are there skilled surf board riders here. Huge waves start breaking a quarter of a mile offshore when a surfer gets started....They sure go fast too. Sometimes one of them falls and the wave tosses the surfboard up in the air. I wish I had time to learn to use one. People rent them and practice but it takes quite a bit of experience. I waded out in the water and expected it to get deeper but found that I could walk two blocks straight out and it stayed chin high except when a big wave rolled in. It is more fun to let a big one take and toss you head over heels, then stand up, rub the salt from your *eyes and wait for the next. I think I'll build a grass hut near the beach and invite Mort or Jack Selden over.*

I also went on a chartered bus. We traveled along the seashore highway. I sent a card to you from the place where we ate dinner. I saw hundreds of acres of pineapples…half grown. We have them served on ship and are they ever good. Remember how I used to hate them?

Next Wednesday we leave the islands for San Pedro. We will stay there five days then go to Bremerton dry dock for three months. We will be at sea until the 17th…so I will not be able to write. Maybe I'll get a chance to see Great Aunt Minnie while at San Pedro.

There will be another mail call before we leave so I hope I get a letter from somebody. I am always glad to hear about the children. Little David has plenty to say now I suppose. If I could only see him. I thought of sending them something for their birthdays but it is hard to send anything here. I'm glad Robert is working more steadily again and hope it keeps on that way.

Ask Grandma Ualia to please wipe the dishes for me and keep her apron pressed!!! Give my love to her and Dad.

Lovingly,
Harry

Letter No. 9: Harry Kramer to his friend Jack Selden
May 6, 1940
From: Pearl Harbor, Honolulu, HI
To: Chippewa Falls, WI

After Harry finished the letter to his mother, he wrote one to Jack Selden. Harry informed Jack of the specific work tasks he had aboard ship. These ranged from shining portholes and cleaning and painting the mess compartment to scrubbing the decks topside and patching holes in the canopies used to cover the decks.

Harry also explained how the *California* had been having trouble keeping pace with the rest of the fleet, as copious amounts of barnacles had attached to the ship's underbelly. The unwanted stowaways had created enough drag to reduce the ship's speed by one-third. To remedy the problem, *California* had been redirected to Bremerton, Washington, for maintenance.[102]

Dear Jack,

This afternoon our division is laying around doing nothing and enjoying the wonderful Hawaiian climate. It's hard to recall the last time I wrote to you but it's been quite a while. It is hard to send letters when we are at sea, especially these naval problems they have been working on. Our ship sails to San Pedro for five days…then dry dock in Bremerton, Washington for the rest of summer. About the time school starts we will leave the yards for fall gunnery practice. I'll never forget the night of April 25ᵗʰ when the fleet neared Honolulu. Just after dark I could see lights on Diamond Head (a large mountain rising from the seashore). About 9:00 PM the whole fleet put on a big searchlight display for the people of the island.

In the morning our ship slowly moved inland…until it arrived at its pier. The aircraft carrier "Yorktown" is anchored a few hundred feet away and planes are always taking off or landing.

Honolulu is six miles away.…Keeps the taxis busy carrying sailors back and forth. The first day here I got liberty and sure did hurry away from the ship. It seems funny to see so many palm trees but they are sure swell and adds to the beauty.

Just received news that the California is to stay till Monday.…Rest of the fleet is to remain indefinitely. And instead of stopping at Long Beach for five days it will only be for a few hours then we proceed to Bremerton. Those extra few days in dock here will give me a chance to catch up on my letters. The bottom of the ship must be pretty bad because on the way over we could not go faster than 14 knots. The rest of the fleet had to slow down so we could stay together. It is hard to believe that just the barnacles would reduce speed. While in Bremerton, not only the bottom will be scraped but the paint on the topside as well. Normally the work is easy on a battleship. There are times when we are required to put in a full day at some task such as carrying crates of food to the store rooms, etc. For quite a while I was detailed to the mess compartment. Here I had to keep the ports shined, sweep down, scrub paint, work and paint, and see that the mess cooks did their part. However, two weeks ago my division petty officer told me to work out in the air on topside. He said I looked too thin…maybe would help to put on some weight. I like the work. We get up at 5:30 AM and scrub the decks before chow at seven. During the rest of the day the division is painting, making rope mats, mending canvas, etc. While in port, large awnings cover every foot of the deck. Lately, I've been busy patching holes. In the time we call our own…we wash clothes, study, write, etc.

Example of a naval searchlight display, circa 1940. *Author's collection.*

Experiencing the powerful and continuous winds of the Nuuanu Pali Lookout for myself, 2017. It was hard to keep one's feet, exactly as Harry described. *Author's collection.*

Golly it will be vacation for you soon. Have you planned anything for summer? I hope you enjoy your new home. How far is it from the high school? You'll have a good chance to use your bike. You ought to build a little radio to carry along! When I get home we'll have to go on a good old camping trip together. Being on the water for long spells, one does get lonesome for the "good earth."

When we reach Bremerton I'll send another letter. Everyone says it's pretty up there.

Say "Hello" to everyone for me.

Aloha,

Harry

————

Letter No. 10: Harry Kramer to his mother, Eva Kramer
June 15, 1940
From: Bremerton, WA
To: Chippewa Falls, WI

On May 10, just days after Harry's last letter, Great Britain's embattled prime minister, Neville Chamberlain, resigned, as Hitler's war machine continued to drive closer to France. Winston Churchill rose to power as the new prime minister. The leadership style of the often stubborn and pugnacious Churchill was seen by many of his countrymen as their best hope to prevent an eventual German land invasion.[103] In his first speech to the House of Commons, Churchill openly displayed his reputation by proclaiming, "I have nothing to offer but blood, toil, tears, and sweat."[104]

Meanwhile, Hitler's list of European conquests continued to grow. Luxembourg collapsed in one day, the Netherlands fell in five and Belgium was overcome in eighteen. By May 15, newspaper reports claimed that France's famed military defense zone, the Maginot Line, had been compromised. The fall of Belgium meant that Germany could strategically bypass the Maginot Line by simply going around it. France was now on the verge of invasion. By June 10, Italy had publicly joined the Axis powers as an ally to Hitler.[105]

Roosevelt was disturbed by the news coming out of Europe and asked Congress to allocate an additional billion dollars "without delay." He argued that the "incredible events" of the past two weeks "required that American defenses be made more certain." After observing Hitler's blitzkrieg war style, Roosevelt was adamant that "speed was needed" in the military and called for the additional funding to be applied toward "aviation and mechanized equipment." In addition, the president requested that Congress grant him permission to "call into active service" anyone serving in the state National Guard or reserve units. Roosevelt sensed that war was likely inevitable, despite opposition from the majority of the American people. Nonetheless, he carefully marketed the request under the guise of "maintaining our position of neutrality" and to "safeguard our national defense."[106]

On Flag Day, June 14, as Harry and the *California* steamed toward Bremerton, Ralph and Eva Kramer read the enlarged headline "Nazis Capture Paris: France on Edge of Complete Disaster."[107] Harry, in his most recent letter, remained silent on the matter. He focused on the complexities of getting enough leave to travel home, as well as his desire to transfer into the ship's machine shop. Tempering any hopeful expectations held by his parents, he reminded them of his lack of seniority onboard. Having sensed his parents' unease about events in France, he reassured them that the *California* was unlikely to visit the East Coast. Now in Bremerton, Harry shared how he enjoyed meeting a couple of people connected to the First Church of Christ, Scientist.[108]

> *Dear Mother,*
>
> *Every time I come to a town I want to write a letter, but you don't mind do you? Tonight I visited the Reading Room in the library. I happened to meet a boy in the ship's library who is also a Church of Christ Scientist member. We just got through reading a lesson. Tomorrow if I can get off at noon I'll go to church here in Bremerton. The lady at the reading room used to live in Wisconsin years ago.*
>
> *Dad's letter came…telling me what he thought about coming home. It's a hard problem to work out. I'd just love to come back but if I only got a couple of weeks it wouldn't be as nice. One of the boys tried to get three weeks but they told him he hadn't been in long enough. A lot of the boys are starting to make requests to be transferred to other divisions and I also want to put in mine. But if I make a request for another division it may hinder my getting leave. However, I'll make out my request for the machine shop and talk to the division officer about a leave in August. I'll be on the same ship as now and it will be perhaps two months before getting my transfer. I can't find out as of yet where we'll go after leaving*

the yards but I doubt if we'll go to the East Coast. As I learn how things develop I'll write immediately.

My trip to Seattle was again postponed but I know for sure I'll go next Saturday.

Love,

Harry

Letter No. 11: Harry Kramer to his father, Ralph Kramer
June 16, 1940
From: Bremerton, Washington
To: Chippewa Falls, WI.

Happy Father's Day
Love and best wishes to the best of (Dads).
Love,
Harry
(Pardon the scratchy pen)

Letter No. 12: Harry Kramer to his friend Jack Selden
July 7, 1940
From: Army & Navy YMCA, 320 Marion Street, Seattle, WA
To: Chippewa Falls, WI

In the weeks leading up to the Fourth of July, France had officially collapsed under Nazism. The newly installed national government, based in the city of Vichy, would take on an authoritarian style and collaborate with the Nazi regime. Hitler celebrated by touring France to survey his prize and posed for a photo with the Eiffel Tower. In response to the takeover, large assortments of French resistance forces rallied around General Charles de Gaulle, a popular soldier and statesman, as the recognized leader of a new Free France movement.[109]

As Germany converged against Great Britain, Japan's foreign minister, Hachirō Arita, warned Western leaders not to upend the status quo in East Asia or the South Seas. He stated that the future of these regions is a "matter of grave concern to Japan." He argued that Japan would enforce

The USS *California* docked at Bremerton, Washington, circa 1940. *U.S. Navy.*

an "Oriental Monroe Doctrine," consisting of an East Asia "uniting under a single sphere," with Japan as the "stabilizing force."[110]

In the United States, the Republican Party held its national convention in Philadelphia. On June 28, the party's delegates chose Wendell Willkie as their nominee for president. The Indiana-born lawyer and corporate executive was a dark horse candidate who directly opposed the isolationist views of challenger Thomas E. Dewey. By contrast, Willkie was an interventionist who supported British aid to fight Hitler. The delegates believed that Willkie was their best chance at outflanking Roosevelt on his political left, as Willkie's progressive views on Black civil rights included the racial integration of the armed forces and civil service apparatuses of the national government.[111]

As for Harry, he anticipated a lengthy stay for the *California* in Bremerton. For sailors eager to get off the ship, the city of Seattle was just a seventeen-mile ferry ride to the east, across Puget Sound. Harry explored all that Seattle had to offer, including the art museum in Volunteer Park and the First Church of Christ, Scientist. Once again, Harry spent time with the "lady in the reading room." She was a librarian named Mildred Grant, whom he referred to as "Mrs. Grant" in future letters. A native of Wisconsin herself, Mildred was a fifty-year-old widow who also was a member of the Church of Christ, Scientist. Their similar geographical and religious connections served as the foundation for a meaningful platonic relationship, as each looked forward to the other's company.[112] Harry also revealed that he had been assigned to "mess cooking," whose responsibilities would hinder his ability to travel back home.[113]

Dear Jack,

My liberty is drawing to a close. I'll leave Seattle on the ferry and return to Bremerton. This has been my second visit to Seattle and know my way around well. I met a nice lady in the reading room who used to live near Chippewa Falls. Last evening we had dinner at one of the big hotels. It was a lot of fun and a good change from the routine of the ship. All of the rooms were taken at the YMCA so I went to a nearby hotel. After going to the First Church of Christ, Scientist, I walked to "Volunteer Park." It is a beautiful place and I was interested in visiting the museum there. A large Chinese collection of paintings and carved ivory was on display. It was almost unbelievable to see how intricate and complicated the patterns were.

Just before leaving, I bought summer pants and a sport shirt. Boy it was a treat to walk around with something cool on. My clothes from home should be here by tomorrow and I'll use them in whatever kind of climate I

One of the sites Harry visited in Seattle, Washington, circa 1940. *Author's collection.*

July Fourth menu aboard
the USS *California*, July 4,
1940. *Author's collection.*

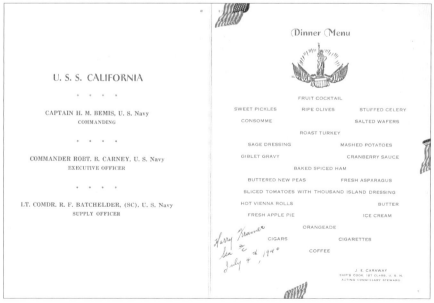

U. S. S. CALIFORNIA

* * * *

CAPTAIN H. M. BEMIS, U. S. Navy
COMMANDING

* * * *

COMMANDER ROBT. B. CARNEY, U. S. Navy
EXECUTIVE OFFICER

* * * *

LT. COMDR. R. F. BATCHELDER, (SC), U. S. Navy
SUPPLY OFFICER

Dinner Menu

FRUIT COCKTAIL

SWEET PICKLES   RIPE OLIVES   STUFFED CELERY
CONSOMME   SALTED WAFERS
ROAST TURKEY
SAGE DRESSING   MASHED POTATOES
GIBLET GRAVY   CRANBERRY SAUCE
BAKED SPICED HAM
BUTTERED NEW PEAS   FRESH ASPARAGUS
SLICED TOMATOES WITH THOUSAND ISLAND DRESSING
HOT VIENNA ROLLS   BUTTER
FRESH APPLE PIE   ICE CREAM
ORANGEADE
CIGARS   CIGARETTES
COFFEE

J. E. CARAWAY
SHIP'S COOK, 1ST CLASS, U. S. N.
ACTING COMMISSARY STEWARD

run into. Two weeks ago…I had a difficult time enjoying myself as it was so hot. Our dress blues are very closely woven and they hold the heat. There are three locker clubs in Bremerton and all of them do a rushing business as most everyone has his own civilian clothes.

As long as I'm on mess cooking I don't believe I'll get leave…perhaps this fall.

I was sorry to hear that your Grandmother is not well. I hope she is better. Tell her "Hello" for me and that I miss…visiting your house. I'll always remember the good things she used to fix.

Your pal,
Harry

Letter No. 13: Harry Kramer to his mother, Eva Kramer
July 12, 1940
From: Bremerton, WA
To: Chippewa Falls, WI

With the Republican ticket for president settled, the Democratic Party faced its own conundrum. Roosevelt was in the final year of a full second term, and no American president had ever served longer than the eight-year tradition set by George Washington. It been reported that Roosevelt was not officially a "candidate for a third term" but that he wouldn't refuse the party nomination if offered. Congressman Adolph Sabath of Chicago, who was an ardent supporter, predicted, "I think I've had a good idea of what's in his mind. He is going to be nominated and re-elected and I will stake my life on it."[114]

The following day, Germany and Italy started the Battle of Great Britain. The specifics of their three-part plan were outlined in an Italian newspaper and republished by the American press: first, "blockade the British Isles"; second, break Britain's "empire contacts"; and finally, defeat "at home, in imperial territories, and at sea." Each Axis power would carry out specific tasks. The United States government, meanwhile, announced it would be taking bids for the construction of 629 new tanks.[115]

In this letter to his mother, Harry gave a maintenance update on *California.* His most recent ship assignment had him making food as part of the "mess men" detail. He also recounted having dinner with Mrs. Grant, attending service at the Church of Christ, Scientist, and sightseeing at the Seattle Art Museum in Volunteer Park.

While the navy had lived up to the adventure and excitement he craved, Harry was ever cognizant that it had come at the expense of lost family moments spent in Chippewa Falls. In particular, he reminisced about playing with his older brother's three young boys, Carl, Gerald and David.[116]

Dear Mother,

Maybe you have been wondering why I'm not sending letters. Well, our ship is in dry dock and I am busier than ever. When the ship was in place the large gate closed and the water slowly lowered. Everyone was equipped with scrapers to remove the barnacles. It was quite an occasion and many people stood around to watch. We even had the ship's orchestra on the quarterdeck… played swing music all evening. We "mess men"…were busy getting ready all the sandwiches and coffee. The men finished about eleven PM and were pretty hungry. The bottom has to be completely scraped to the steel plating and given several paint jobs. The galley is also being repaired. The laundry is not in use and I am kept busy scrubbing clothes…after supper.

I stopped in at the locker club and found that the clothes were waiting for me. You said that you did not send the green gabardine pants. Sometime later could you please wrap and mail them to the same address?

I went to Seattle again and had a swell time. I called Mrs. Grant and we had supper at one of the nice hotels. Sunday after church I walked out a few blocks further and visited Volunteer Park. It is a wonderful spot and the Seattle Art Museum is located there.

I hope all of you folks had a pleasant 4th. I was on the ship but boy did we have the food. Will send you one of the menus.

I sure laughed when you wrote about my nephew Carl saying, "Some folks do" when telling him he couldn't shoot the firecrackers until the 4th. They sure can figure things out quick…for their age. Boy I'd give anything to see and play with the kids again.

Several days ago I found six dollars. It was a surprise and I waited to have someone call for it…but no one has. Whenever anything is lost on ship, the loser always puts a slip on the main bulletin board…seen by a majority of the crew. I could never find anyone losing that much money. I still wonder where it came from.

Well, I'd better get some sleep. Hope everyone is well. Give my love to Grandma Ualia and Dad.

Love,

Harry

Letter No. 14: Harry Kramer to his mother, Eva Kramer
August 1, 1940
From: Bremerton, WA
To: Chippewa Falls, WI

In the weeks following Hitler's conquest of France, the Vichy government passed a series of xenophobic and anti-Semitic laws that mirrored those in Germany. They revoked French citizenship from all naturalized Jews and forbade employment to any resident not born to French parents.[117]

For Roosevelt, the delegates at the Democratic Party's national convention, in Chicago, had overwhelmingly nominated him for a third term. Joining him on ticket was Henry Wallace, an Iowa-born former Republican who had served as his secretary of agriculture since 1932. The Roosevelt/Wallace ticket was a formidable one. Speaking from the White House via radio broadcast, Roosevelt reminded everyone that only the American people could decide who won. He did warn, however, that during this time of "public danger," now was not the time for "untried, inexperienced hands."[118]

The next day, July 19, Hitler gave a speech to the Reichstag that included a direct warning to Great Britain and Churchill. Hitler warned that they could either make peace now or face their own destruction. He foretold that "a world empire would be destroyed" between them but that the loser wouldn't be Germany.[119]

While American support for isolationism remained strong, there was growing skepticism regarding Great Britain's ability to defend itself. Members of Congress even began discussions on instituting a peacetime military draft. Roosevelt's secretary of the treasury, Henry Morgenthau, announced that Great Britain would be purchasing three thousand U.S.-built airplanes per month. He added that the British had promised to pay for the construction of new factories and buy the output from each. "The British seem to have plenty of money," he assured members of the press. "The sums involved are colossal."[120]

In Bremerton, the USS *California* remained dry-docked. Harry did mention the proposed peacetime draft bill, as well as alterations the ship would need if war was necessary. As far as Harry knew, the ship was still on schedule to return to the Pacific Fleet at Pearl Harbor. He also took time to reflect on various happenings pertaining to people he knew back home. He had been surprised to hear the wedding announcement of William "Bill" Howie and Alice "Vernie" Zenner, who were two friends from high school.[121] He also verbalized his appreciation for recent letters received from Jack Selden and Marie Kramer, his sister-in-law. Harry chuckled as he contemplated any resemblance between his older brother and his one-year-old nephew, David.

Harry also revealed how thoughtful and kind-hearted he was. He inquired into the health of Jack Selden's paternal grandmother, Ida Gailey, and daydreamed about life back in Chippewa Falls while on leave. He desperately wanted to eat his favorite homemade foods and revel in the companionship of his family. What Harry seemed to want most, however, was to have his very own kitten to spend time with.[122] He even asked his mother if, when he was on leave, he could drive out to the farm of Henry and Frances Buske to pick one up.[123]

Dear Mother,

After a shave, shine, shampoo, and shower, I feel just in the right mood to answer your wonderful letter. It certainly was a long one but we like them that way. I get mail moments before the noon meal and I have the problem of eating a sandwich, reading the letters, and running the chow line all at the same time.

It sure put me back on my heels…about Bill Howie. Boy I thought my eyes were deceiving…Read the article five times. Never dreamed he would get married so soon. Do you know what work he's been doing?

I received a letter from Marie and one from Jack Selden. I love to hear about the hometown. Marie sent a picture of David and boy do I prize that. He looks better than ever and how I'd like to be back there playing with him and the others. I got a kick out of David holding the newspaper as his Dad was doing. He has always been smart and quick. Well haven't they all!

Our ship is gradually being finished. On one of the bulletin boards is posted a huge chart where the percentage of work done on each individual job is marked…and estimated cost is recorded. I was amazed to see how expensive it is to repair a ship. For instance, the main and quarterdecks will cost eighty thousand dollars…quite a bit of cash. And to think if the USA declared war it would all have to be torn up and removed… and our steel lockers and bunks taken out. That is to prevent loose things flying around. But I hope the day never arrives. I notice a bill is before Congress, which would require the younger men to undergo a period of military service.

I believe it is definite that the USS California will return to Hawaiian waters. The time set to leave the yards is August 27th. Two or three new range finder turrets are under construction up on the masts and it seems like they have an awful lot to do yet. It is interesting to note how some of the work is done. The old deck was held down by means of bolts thru the steel plating. When this was torn up and all those hundreds of bolts taken out, the overhead looked like a sieve. I had a hard time setting up my mess as the dirt from above sometimes came pouring down. Finally, however, all these were welded. Now the deck is secured in a new way.

We are always late in setting up for noon chow, as the pay lines don't get through until 11:30. I got four dollars in tips though. I get the weekend off again…so will use the spare cash. I got acquainted with a marine from La Crosse, Wisconsin and if he'd have had this weekend off too, we'd rent some bikes and take a trip in the country. He went two weeks ago and said it was swell scenery. However, if I don't find someone else that I know well to go with, then I'll probably end up in Seattle.

As I lay in my bunk last night I was thinking that had I gone home on leave in July it would all be over now. But I still can look forward to it can't I? Let's see, I'll have pancakes for breakfast, strawberry shortcake, and ice cream at noon and nut bread, mashed potatoes, meat and gravy, and grape juice for supper. Did I miss anything? O yes, I'd have the kiddies down to help eat too. Another thing, now that Dad has the car I could go out to Buske's farm and borrow a kitten for the month's leave couldn't I? You know how I always wanted one.

I'm so happy to learn that Mrs. Gailey is feeling better. Tell Grandma Ualia thanks for her letter and I like it a lot. Am glad all of you are well and getting along OK.

Love,
Harry

Letter No. 15: Harry Kramer to his friend Jack Selden
August 16, 1940
From: Bremerton, WA
To: Chippewa Falls, WI

As a summer of global unrest transitioned to fall, only Great Britain stood in the way of Germany's complete conquest of Western Europe. Hitler's invasion of the island was scheduled for less than a month away. Code-named Operation Sealion, the strategy called for Nazi foot soldiers to invade the mainland and capture London. Prior to this, Germany would need to destroy Great Britain's Royal Air Force. Hitler ordered his Luftwaffe, the German air force, to bomb Great Britain's ports and airfields. Compounding Britain's concerns, media reports suggested a diplomatic break between Britain and Japan was also near.[124]

The reality of destroying Churchill's air power proved difficult. Britain continued aerial assaults and bombings raids throughout Germany, inflicting major destruction in Hamburg, Bremen and Cologne.[125] As both a leader and a symbol, Churchill was a formidable force. A photo of him holding an American Thompson submachine gun circulated on the front pages of American newspapers. In the photo, Churchill wore a pinstripe suit and black top hat; a six-inch Romeo y Julieta cigar was firmly clenched within his partial grin. The caption read: "Inspection of Coastal Defenses."[126]

This not-so-subtle attempt to rally support from the American people was not lost on retired army general John J. Pershing. Having led U.S. soldiers against Germany in World War I, Pershing called on the American people to come to Britain's aid before it was too late. Pershing saw "grave danger" for the United States if Britain fell and called on the U.S. government to "make ourselves strong" by building up "our army and navy." Pershing advocated for a peacetime military draft and called for the administration to send fifty American destroyers to Britain.[127]

But isolationism from global affairs was still a popular position among Americans. Speaking to a crowd of forty thousand supporters of the Citizens Keep America Out of War Committee at Soldier Field in Chicago, famed aviator Charles Lindbergh called for peace and cooperation. He predicted a future where "we may have to deal with a Europe dominated by Germany," rather than "England and France," but one in which the United States would still be the leader of the Western Hemisphere, regardless of the outcome in Europe.[128]

In Washington, D.C., Roosevelt was incensed by the advances made by Japan in China. Now the Japanese were angling to occupy parts of French Indochina, per an agreement with the new Vichy government in France. In response to past aggressions, Roosevelt froze all Japanese assets in the United States and placed an oil embargo on aviation gasoline to countries outside the Western Hemisphere. Other allies followed Roosevelt's lead, resulting in a 75 percent reduction in Japan's foreign trade, including an 88 percent hit to its imported oil. Japan's war machine was starving.[129]

While global events escalated, the USS *California* was nearing the end of its dry dock stay in Bremerton. As Harry's seniority grew, so did opportunities to work in more coveted positions. In this letter, Harry discussed his move to the ship's freshwater hold, located in the bow of the ship. The hold's fresh water was used to cool the ship's boilers and as a potable water source for the crew. Harry was more suited for this work, as he possessed an aptitude for working with the pumps, pipes, gauges and valves. It also placed him deep within the bowels of the vessel, far below the ship's waterline.

During his last days in Washington State, Harry visited some remaining sites in Seattle. He attended church at another Church of Christ, Scientist building, indulged himself in a large piece of wild blackberry pie at the famous and touristy Home of the Green Apple Pie Restaurant and napped under a tree in the city's ever-popular Woodland Park. As a young man whose childhood was defined by the Great Depression, Harry was both appreciative and grateful for the life he was now living.

Nonetheless, Harry did lament about missing the Northern Wisconsin State Fair (NWSF) in Chippewa Falls. First held in 1897, the NWSF constituted the largest annual gathering of people in the region. With tens of thousands in attendance, the fair was a multiday affair that included farm animal judging, educational exhibits, carnival rides, horse-pulling competitions, midwestern eats and a lighted midway filled with games and shows. The large grandstand provided an assortment of family-friendly entertainment, including vaudeville acts such as comedies, songs and dancing girls, mixed in with fancy costumes and elaborate light shows. That year's "brilliant musical extravaganza" was entitled "Star Brigade," which was reported as having been "greatly received" by the audience.[130]

On Friday, the fair hosted what it called "Thrill Day," so named after the death-defying daredevil and stunt automobile show that afternoon, called "The Flash Williams Thrill Show." Despite all the happenings, it was Irene Bernier who made front-page news by setting the NWSR's cow-milking record. The paper exclaimed, "Before a big bandstand crowd…Mrs. Irene Bernier…coaxed her cow to the new record of 16 and 1/10 pounds of milk…in a three-minute period."[131] The fair was a time for family, friends and the proud celebration of living life in Wisconsin.[132]

But then Harry remembered the cold winters back home and quipped that he would be trading that for the pain of getting a Hawaiian sunburn.[133]

Dear Jack,

Perhaps you got a chance to read mother's letter recently.…I've been transferred to "A" Division. A week ago someone came up and said, "I heard that you are going down below today." I was surprised and pleased as I had been told…they were not sending anyone from the deck force until the ship left the yards. The next morning I was shown my new quarters and lockers. It took nearly an hour to get all my clothes and bedding squared away. Just before dinner the junior officer of the division, Ensign O'Brian, told me to help out in the motor launches the rest of the day. Boy I was sure happy to work around the diesel motors...close to the water. About 4 PM one of the engineers had to make a trip across the bay and pick up men on liberty. He took me along, explaining how everything worked. On the way over I learned the bell code. 1 bell—ahead, 2 bells—stop, 3 bells—reverse, and 4 bells— full speed ahead. All an engineer has to do is keep his ears open...shift gears and change speed to conform with the coxswain's orders. On our return trip... he told me to take over as we neared the dock. Well, I sure had a lot of fun running the motor. After that I got a chance to run the launch twice a day... and a little later had my own boat to handle alone. For four days, I helped clean up the launches in-between the trips and when there was no work to do we'd go up to the boat shack...drink coffee, read magazines and talk.

Last week, I was put on a new job. That of being in the fresh water hold. I'm still there. This hold is in the forward part of the ship, ten feet below sea level. There is a single room here containing five bilge electric pumps, numerous pipelines and dozens of valves of all sizes. I am studying these things and will gradually learn to operate the fresh water system. Considering the watches you have to stand, it is about the best job on the ship. I've been very busy helping to clean out each of the six tanks surrounding us. Altogether they hold approximately a hundred thousand gallons of water. At the moment, the USS California is returning from a trial run, so the tanks had to be in readiness for this trip. While tied up at the docks, water is taken directly from the yard's water line...so our pumps aren't used. This morning at 3:45 AM the ship was ready to pull out so the other boy, who is my boss, stayed up to fill all the tanks. Yesterday someone drained the water for the boilers by mistake and we had to pump twenty thousand gallons more before the hose on the dock was disconnected. However, everything was filled just in time, and the two of us hurried to our bunks. Don't try shaving and showering at 3 AM if you haven't had any sleep. I put toothpaste on my shaving brush—ah, me! After next week when things are cleaned up we won't have anything to do except watch the pumps and gauges. There is a swell steel desk where you can write or study. I also have the use of an electric iron...to keep my clothes in good shape.

The ship is now back at the dock, ready to tie up for ten days, then back to Honolulu, after a three-day stopover at San Pedro. It doesn't look as if I'll get leave. If I do get a chance to come home in winter, I'll guess my plans for a

Matchbooks featuring some of the places Harry visited in Washington State, circa 1940. *Author's collection.*

camping trip will be shot. Oh well, maybe when the snow is flying back home, I'll be sun burning myself on the sandy beach of Waikīkī.

You have been to the fair I suppose? It seems rather funny to me, not to see any of these things this time of year. Mort wrote saying that the grandstand performance was pretty good this year.

Say it suddenly dawned on me that you'll be going to school again. Boy the time sure flies, especially on vacation. Your next three years at high school will be enjoyable...a lot of varied courses and nice shops to work in. I wish I were going to high school again.

My boss just came down...and was quite certain I'd stay here on this work. He has a lot of good books which I can study...and it is a good station in which to become acquainted with many of the officers, as so many phone calls and reports have to be handled.

When I arrived in Seattle I got a room again at the YMCA and began a tour around town. It sure is pretty at night with all the neon signs and window displays. At twelve o'clock I was back in my cozy room and ready to sleep. I decided to get up around seven thirty in the morning and put in a good day at sightseeing. Well, Saturday morning came and when I'd dressed and was walking down the hall I asked a boy what time it was. He said, "Ten to twelve." Boy oh boy, I nearly fell over. I'm in the habit of always waking up about six o'clock but the bed must have been too comfortable for I never opened an eye until I got up. Although my start was a bit behind, I had a swell day as usual. I ate at a famous restaurant called "Home of the Green Apple Pie." It achieved fame because of the wonderful homemade pies. The couple who started the place...has branched out into a big business. I ordered wild blackberry pie a la mode. You can imagine how good that was. They give you a darned big piece too. Sunday, I went to the Fourth Church of Christ Scientist and enjoyed it very much. In the afternoon I had a swell time out at Woodland Park. There was a big crowd there and everyone seemed happy. I stretched out beneath some big trees as many others were doing and went to sleep for an hour while taking in the scenery around me. It was good to be near the "good earth" again after spending so many days on the ship.

I've been writing your letter down here in the fresh water hold and it sure is nice. I'm all by myself and have a comfortable stool and desk to use. This evening I cleaned out a big steel locker near the desk and moved a lot of my things from above. Now I have plenty of spare room and it makes it easier to keep my things clean and wrinkle proof. My liking for this station grows day by day. Can't think of anything more...will close with a wave and farewell!
Your water-logged friend,
Harry

Letter No. 16: Harry Kramer to his friend Jack Selden
September 2, 1940
From: Pearl Harbor, Honolulu, Hawaii
To: Chippewa Falls, WI

While work was completed on *California*, Germany initiated its naval blockade of Great Britain. Hitler ordered his troops to be amassed in ports along the French side of the English Channel as he waited impatiently for his air forces to create an opening. In the meantime, Hitler announced to the world that vessels from neutral nations would be fought at "full blast" as the whole region was "infested with mines" and "airplanes." As the Battle of Britain entered its third month, Churchill's Royal Air Force had successfully bombed the German capital of Berlin. In retaliation, Hitler bombed London.[134]

With the presidential election three months away, Roosevelt juggled the country's desire for isolationism with his own view that the United States needed to do more. Media reports of Britain's desire for an "Arms Alliance with the US" only complicated matters. Roosevelt's Republican challenger, Wendell Willkie, took notice and accused Roosevelt of purposely courting war. He argued that Roosevelt "secretly meddled in the affairs of Europe" and was pushing toward a war that America was "hopelessly unprepared for" and "emphatically did not want." Willkie concluded that the administration "cannot lead you to victory against Hitler, or against anyone else."[135]

Undeterred by the criticism, Roosevelt pushed Congress to pass a selective service act. Roosevelt hoped that enacting a peacetime draft would increase the country's military ranks from 400,000 to 1,200,000. Ironically, Willkie endorsed the plan. While Congress debated the specifics of the draft issue, Roosevelt used his constitutional powers to elevate 60,000 National Guardsmen to federal service.[136]

Harry and the crew of the USS *California* left Bremerton, barnacle-free, and sailed back to Hawaii. Harry shared details about the "war games" he participated in, as well as sleep-related challenges relating to his work schedule in the freshwater hold. He also was thrilled to be back on Waikiki Beach.[137]

Dear Jack,

I am back in Hawaii. The USS California stopped at Long Beach… during which I visited my relatives and had a wonderful weekend. On the return trip from La Jolla, California, where my Great Aunt Minnie lives, we passed Bing Crosby's race track. There was a huge crowd waiting to see the events. That night my cousin and I went on a treasure hunt with some of his friends. Next morning, our ship began its six day crossing to join the rest of the fleet. All the while we practiced war games and drills. Under these conditions a person never knows when he'll hear general quarters—or battle stations. It may be one or two o'clock in the morning and a guy always hates to have his sleep interrupted. One night…near Lahaina Roads, a cruiser cut across our path only a few yards ahead of the bow. Each ship sighted one another at the last moment before hitting. I didn't know anything about this until the next day. A few days later the

USS Yorktown and a submarine had an accident. The sub came up under the aircraft carrier by mistake breaking off her periscope and flooding a compartment. I don't know if anyone was hurt.

After a few days of maneuvers, the fleet anchored in Pearl Harbor for nine days rest. The ship tied up about 400 feet off shore as no docks were available. We stretched a fire hose across the distance to receive fresh water in the ship's tanks. The water was turned on each night at ten o'clock and secured at 6 AM. There are just two of us on this station…so every other night I would have to stay awake and regulate the pressure. It was hard to stay up sometimes.

I went to Honolulu three times and had wonderful liberties. When not swimming at Waikīkī, I spent many happy hours walking up and down the seashore, visiting parks, hunting souvenirs and enjoying the swell scenery. It is surprising how many of the crew hate being out here or going into Honolulu. I'm getting so I like it.

I've been thinking about you going to high school. How are you getting along? Boy I wish I were sitting in one of those classes again. I miss school an awful lot.

The mail closes in five minutes so I will try to get this in the box in time. Send best wishes to all.

Your pal,

Harry

––––––––

Letter No. 17: Harry Kramer to his mother, Eva Kramer
October 6, 1940
From: Pearl Harbor, Honolulu, HI
To: Chippewa Falls, WI

In the month since Harry last wrote, global events had led to the near collapse of Great Britain. Hitler scheduled his land invasion of Great Britain for September 21, as Britain rushed to acquire fifty overage U.S. Navy destroyers from the Roosevelt administration. In exchange, the United States received lease rights to numerous British naval and air installations in the Atlantic Ocean, including Newfoundland and several spots in the Caribbean Sea.[138] The trade made strategic sense for both leaders, as Churchill needed hardware while Roosevelt sought to shore up defenses in the Western Hemisphere.[139]

Knowing that Roosevelt would face political pushback from his detractors—and during a reelection year, no less—Churchill marketed the trade as a way for America to "avoid the danger." He also told Parliament that America was "still not in the war." He did admit, however, that "there is no doubt that Hitler will not like this transference of destroyers."[140] Days later, Hitler commenced bombings over London and other cities across England. Instead of just hitting military targets, the Blitz called for "terror raid" bombings, purposely designed to inflict suffering and death on civilians. In the coming months, over one million homes and flats would be destroyed and forty-three thousand civilians killed.[141]

With the presidential election a month out, Roosevelt was hit hard by criticism and consternation from isolationists. A Gallup poll showed their strength, as 48 percent of Americans wanted Roosevelt to "keep out" of Europe. This culminated in the formation of one of the largest isolationist and antiwar organizations in American history. Formed on Yale University's campus, the America First Committee favored strong defenses at home while maintaining a neutral foreign policy. At its peak, the group claimed 450 chapters and ballooned to a national membership of 800,000. Its members included prominent citizens, including famed aviator Charles Lindbergh and silent-screen actress Lillian Gish.[142] Almost immediately, the group was accused of embracing overtones of anti-Semitism and Nazi sympathizing. In one speech, Lindbergh argued that the "greatest threat to this country lies in the [Jewish] large ownership and influence in our motion pictures, our press, our radio and our government." An appalled Wendell Willkie surmised that Lindbergh had given "the most un-American talk made in my time by any person of national reputation."[143]

Despite the meteoric rise of America First, Roosevelt and Congress continued to ready America's capabilities. Authorized by a recently signed defense appropriation measure, the navy quickly awarded contracts for the construction of 201 new warships.[144] Three days later, Manitowoc Shipbuilding Corporation in Wisconsin was informed it would construct ten new submarines. Even the Chippewa Falls Woolen Mill Company, situated on the banks of Duncan Creek in Harry's hometown, secured $125,000 to produce "overcoating" for future military draftees.[145]

Then, on September 14, Congress approved a peacetime military draft. Over sixteen million men, aged twenty-one to thirty-six, would register. Pending the president's signature, military leaders anticipated the first seventy-five thousand draftees would arrive in boot camps by November.[146] Speaking at a Teamsters' Union event, Roosevelt reaffirmed his commitment to keeping America out of war. "I hate war now more than ever," the president exclaimed. "I have one supreme determination—to do all that I can to keep war away from these shores for all time."[147]

The next day, September 15, Churchill's Royal Air Force scored a major and decisive aerial victory against Hitler's Luftwaffe on what's now commemorated as Battle of Britain Day. The RAF inflicted big losses on Germany's two massive waves of bombing raids. With Hitler's air forces depleted, his invasion of mainland Britain was halted.[148] Undeterred, Hitler and Mussolini met in Rome to discuss the plausibility of Spain joining their alliance by bribing the Spanish with the spoils of Gibraltar and French Morocco as a reward.[149]

Days after Britain's victory, Japan marched into French Indochina. An infuriated Roosevelt said he "would not let this go unchallenged" and hinted that "warships may be sent to the region."[150] Three days later, without referencing Japan, Roosevelt announced that all scrap iron and steel shipments would be halted to any country outside of the Western Hemisphere, excluding Great Britain. The move deprived Japan of key supplies to build its war machine. In response, Japan announced it would "actively support" Germany if the United States entered the European war. On September 27, Japan signed the Tripartite Agreement with Germany and Italy, thus joining the Axis powers.[151] In an article titled "Japanese Press Sees Clash with America," a Tokyo newspaper predicted, "It now seems inevitable that a clash [will take place] between a Japan determined to establish a sphere of self-sufficiency and a United States equally determined to meddle in affairs on the other side of a vast ocean with every hostile means short of war."[152]

The beginning of October saw the arrival of the first batch of overage naval destroyers to Great Britain, as well as the finalization of U.S. citizenship for a German-born Jewish scientist named Albert Einstein. For Harry and the crew of *California*, a fever epidemic that had broken out during war games forced them to anchor away from the fleet in Lahaina. Harry described the live-firing drills on the ship, as well as his excitement for the "new uniforms" the soldiers could wear.

Harry also ran into a familiar face in Honolulu, as John "Jack" Larson had recognized him on his way back to the ship. John graduated high school with Harry and joined up earlier in 1939. He was stationed aboard the USS *Paul Jones*, a destroyer assigned to the Asiatic Fleet. It had stopped in Pearl Harbor on its way back to the Philippines, in East Asia.[153] John's older brother, Emery Larson, served aboard the USS *Tennessee*, *California's* sister ship. Harry had crossed paths with him, too, back in Bremerton.[154] The Larson boys had grown up not far from the Kramers, in a two-story house located at 118 East Cedar Street. The Larson house was centrally located near the downtown, just a block away from the Chippewa Falls Woolen Mill and Leinenkugel Brewing Company. Harry knew that several boys from Depression-era Chippewa Falls had enlisted, and he was eager to see each of them.[155]

In this letter, Harry discussed the health and happenings of specific people in Wisconsin. Henryietta Buske, of Anson Township, had undergone a medical procedure, and Gordon Howie had been hospitalized after being hit by a motorist while working with the county highway crew in Eagleton.[156] But not all the news was concerning. Florence Cook, the wife of Chippewa County judge Dayton Cook, had recently purchased new books and manuals for the youth at Harry's church. Like the Kramers, the Cooks were devout followers of the Church of Christ, Scientist. By contrast, the Cooks were one of the wealthiest families in Chippewa Falls and lived in the city's most historic and well-known mansion from the logging era, the Cook-Rutledge Mansion. The Cooks were also helping the church construct a new building, located just down the street from their home.[157]

Dear Mother,

I heard mail call go and that's sweet music to anyone's ears. Boy it took me two seconds to grab your air mail letter, run up two decks and spread myself gracefully on the forecastle in preparation to read all about a little hamlet, of Chippewa Falls, four thousand miles away! And how I enjoyed those wonderful pages. Dad wrote such a nice letter too. Give my nephew Carl a big hug for his splendid drawing. I'm going to start a scrapbook… and his work will hold a prominent position among its pages. It will be a happy day when I can see all the children again.

Perhaps you received my short letter written at the YMCA in Honolulu. Well on the way back to the ship I met Jack Larson. He came up and slapped me on the back. I was very much surprised. I had seen his brother, Emery, on my first trip to Seattle. We didn't get to talk very long as my motor launch came and I had to go. Eventually, I believe I'll bump into all the boys from Chippewa Falls.

On September 23rd most of the fleet left Pearl Harbor for war games. Our ship along with two others had to give up drills and pull in at Lahaina…as a fever epidemic broke out. We anchored here six days until it cleared. I felt very well all the while. During all these maneuvers the turret crews for the twelve big fourteen inch guns only pretended to shoot off in practice, training them on other ships. Last Friday, was a day set aside for actual firing drills.

Sailors at Lahaina on the Island of Maui, Hawaii, circa 1940. *Author's collection.*

I'd never heard one of those big guns go off so I was curious to see how much noise they made. Everyone had to stay clear of the main deck and all hatches were closed. I was in the fresh water hold but could hear over the loudspeaker as they called ready for firing. Finally, there was a "boom" and the steel bilge plates which I was standing on, shook like a grizzly trying to shake off old age. Then all morning long it kept up until one o'clock. They shot short range at a target towed by a destroyer. I don't know how many hits were scored but 75, sixteen hundred-pound shells were used, costing around a hundred thousand dollars, so I was told.

Oh yes, the Navy is giving us new uniforms! Each man has to take two pairs of white pants and have them snipped off above the knees! In other words...shorts. I've already had my pants made up. Boy, it will look funny at first and everyone has been talking over the situation. We will start wearing them in a couple of weeks. They'll be nice and cool...I wish we were using them now.

You spoke about the books Mrs. Cook said they were ordering. That is certainly nice giving away a book to the students. I would like a manual, though I believe I would enjoy any one of the others. I will try to send Mrs. Cook a letter.

I was very surprised about Mr. Howie. It's unfortunate that he had to be injured...and lay up from work. How are the rest of the family? Bill & Grace in particular. Has Bill any work yet? If you see Mrs. Buske...give her my regards and...wish her a speedy recovery.

Every day I imagine I'm back home…and going to the river for a swim, hiking up along the swamp to the dam, or walking downtown, visiting people, etc. It is nice and warm out here but I'm going to miss that snow. Remember when Mort and I went down to the swamp in the midst of a blizzard, and made beef steak sandwiches by a little fire from the back of a tree? That was the life. I sure miss Mort and can hardly wait to see the scamp again!

My bunk is calling me and will quickly comply with its wishes! I'm glad you are all well and thanks for the wonderful letter.

Love to all,

Harry

————

Letter No. 18: Harry Kramer to his mother, Eva Kramer
October 27, 1940
From: Pearl Harbor, Honolulu, HI
To: Chippewa Falls, WI

News of Japan's Axis alliance reverberated in the Western world, as the treaty deteriorated Japanese relations with Great Britain and the United States. Churchill—who, months earlier, had closed the Burma Road under Japanese diplomatic pressure—reopened the artery. Constructed in 1937, the road connected the British colony of Burma to the southwestern portion of China. The 717-mile road, used to transport various goods and supplies, was instrumental in China's staving off its Japanese invaders. In response, Japan warned that if the road was reopened, it would be bombed. Japanese news reports surmised that Britain's decision was "an unmistakable indication that she is taking up with the United States a common front against this country."[158]

The temperature of the rhetoric also rose in the United States, as former admiral Harry Yarnell, who once served as commander of the U.S. Navy's Asiatic Fleet, suggested that the United States was "better prepared with a showdown with Japan now, while she is bogged down in China." He feared that waiting too long would allow Japan to enhance its naval power. Reporters from the Associated Press quickly reached out to Secretary of the Navy Frank Knox for a response. Knox said, "No comment." When asked if the rumors were true that Roosevelt expected war with Japan, Knox replied, "No." He added, "I don't believe anybody knows." Knox did say that the Pacific Fleet was being "groomed" and to expect an additional 4,200 men to be added, in order to increase warship capabilities from 85 percent strength to 100 percent.[159]

With the election weeks away, Roosevelt campaigned in places that were billed as part of a "national defense tour," including Pittsburgh's industrial section in eastern Pennsylvania. Roosevelt closed his campaign by emphasizing the need for national defense. By contrast, Republican Wendell Willkie expressed his concerns that the president would "do something or say something" that would trigger a war. If reelected, Willkie warned, Roosevelt's domestic policy failures would be a preview of future foreign policy mistakes.[160]

While Harry avoided discussion of current events in his letters, he broached the topic of the recently instated peacetime draft. He was eager to know if one of his best friends, Mortimer Anderson, who had recently turned twenty-one, had registered yet. Mort, as he was known, was Harry's closest friend from high school. Unlike Jack Selden, Mort grew up in the neighborhood, living a few houses down at 120 Division Street.

Harry's letter also talked about his experiences in Hawaii. He vividly described the lavishness of Honolulu's famed Royal Hawaiian Hotel. Built in 1927 in a Spanish-Moorish style, the six-story, pink, four-hundred-room structure was inspired by scenes from Rudolph Valentino's Arabian movies. The luxurious hotel was a mainstay for celebrities and dignitaries, as its private beach and lounge chairs offered the best vantage point for swimming and sunbathing on Waikiki Beach.[161] In addition to the hotel, the army and navy's YMCA building had drawn his attention, as the venue hosted acts featuring musical acts, comedy shows and other live stage performances.[162]

Dear Mother,

Here I am at the YMCA in Honolulu eagerly awaiting another sing song program. Another boy and I came over this morning and we've been on the go all day. Spent all afternoon around Waikīkī Beach. There was a band concert in a park....We stayed for that. You would think by this stationery that I've been living at the Royal Hawaiian Hotel. Well, hardly as it costs nearly twenty dollars a day. This evening we walked in through the gate to look the grounds over. It's hard to write about because you think you're in dreamland. The lawns are like golf course greens, with giant hedges, flowers, pools, and lots of palms. We then strolled past a ritzy cocktail lounge, and went into the main lobby. Boy oh boy talk about class. On one side there was a large glass enclosed room filled with expensive souvenirs. *Across from it were writing tables and that is where we picked up this stationery. I thought I'd write on it so you could keep it as a souvenir. From one end of the lobby we walked out where many swell tables were being prepared for a dinner party under the stars. The seashore is only a hundred feet away so it sure makes a nice setting. We made our exit, having the stationery and a memory of the place I'll always keep.*

October 30—I went to that sing song so I still haven't finished this. The program at the "Y" was even better than the last. Being Navy Day we sang songs dealing with military life. There were several special entertainers. A girl played a piano accordion and sang popular songs. Then a lady got up and sang about "navy beans." It was comical and her voice would purposely go off tune, with hilarious results. One of the professional troupes put on a hula show. These people could sure sing and I like to listen to the Hawaiian language. Three of the girls…picked out a sailor and dragged him onto stage to try to teach him to do their dance. They tried all right.… Was sure funny.

I got your last letter and it was interesting. You always make me feel so good when I get news concerning the younger set [Harry's nephews]. *So Carl has a bike. Can he ride well? I wish I could watch him. Some time when he is drawing, ask him if he'll send me another. It won't be long before David will be using a pencil.*

It is still just as hot here and the crew are looking forward to leaving for the states. Our stay in Long Beach will last two weeks then the ship heads toward Bremerton again. The ship is to be fitted with special cable running clear around it, which will make magnetic mines ineffective. The weather will certainly be different then here. I'll have to dig out my pea coat. I miss our climate back home. This will be the first Christmas without snow.

Has Mort been around? I suppose he had to register for the draft. We've been seeing much about it in the papers. Tell Mort hello and give my love to Grandma Ualia and Dad.

Love,
Harry

P.S. I enjoyed the cartoon about the sailors. It will be a nice addition to my scrapbook.

Letter No. 19: Harry Kramer to his mother, Eva Kramer
December 18, 1940
From: Pearl Harbor, Honolulu, HI
To: Chippewa Falls, WI

On Tuesday, October 29, President Roosevelt presided over the opening rounds of the Selective Service's draft lottery. A fishbowl containing nine thousand opaque blue capsules, each containing a serial number ranging from 1 to 9,000, was stirred using a wooden spoon made from an old beam taken from Independence Hall in Philadelphia. One by one, each capsule was drawn, and the serial number was read and documented. Seventeen hours and thirty-one minutes later, the bowl was bare. Of the seventeen million registered men, aged twenty-one to thirty-six, the first thirty thousand would be in boot camp within twenty days. Overall, the Selective Service law authorized five million to be conscripted, if needed, by 1945. The plan was to have eight hundred thousand draftees in the ranks by June.[163]

The first serial number drawn was 158. One Chippewa Falls man had "won the lottery." Twenty-seven-year-old Kenneth A. Christianson, who operated a sign business out of his home, located at 1 A Street, owned the unlucky number.[164] Harry's good friend Mort Anderson, who had been given serial number 696, had his number selected on the 1,085[th] draw.[165] Harry's older brother, Robert, was drawn 268th.[166]

With the first two thousand rounds expected to be called up within twelve months, theoretically, all three men could be expected to serve. Limited numbers of draft deferments were available, as long as the registrant had either a dependent, a physical disability or an occupation deemed "essential." Kenneth and Mort did not qualify. Twenty-nine-year-old Robert Kramer was deferred for having three children. Kenneth ended up serving as a private first class in the United States Army. Mort, however, contemplated enlistment in the Army Air Corps in order to bypass being drafted into the infantry.[167]

Exactly one week after the draft selection, the voters of the United States overwhelmingly reelected Roosevelt to a record-setting third term. A record turnout gave Roosevelt 54.7 percent of the popular vote and 449 electoral votes from 38 states. Wendell Willkie received 44.8 percent of the popular vote and won only 82 electoral votes from 10 states. Roosevelt won Wisconsin, but only by 1.83 percent. The rural areas favored Willkie, while urban areas went for Roosevelt. In Harry's Chippewa County, Willkie beat the president by a 10 percent margin.[168]

With the election behind him, Roosevelt continued preparing the United States for the possibility of war, while assisting Great Britain any way he could. Roosevelt announced that the British would be allowed to purchase twelve thousand U.S.-built warplanes, in addition to the fourteen thousand it had already ordered. Roosevelt stated that he was operating on a "rule of thumb policy," whereby Britain and Canada would be supplied 50 percent of American defense items rolling off factory lines. By December 6, the country was adding "new fighting ships to the fleet" at a rate of "one every twelve days."[169] The president revealed that he had been in discussions with Mexico's leader, with a mindset to work together to keep North America free from threats.[170]

In Europe, Germany's loss during the Battle of Britain hadn't slowed its determination. Britain, too, continued to give Germany as good as it got, by bombing Nazi targets in Germany, France and other regions. Around this time, news reports out of Poland began highlighting Hitler's inhumane treatment of Jews. Articles like "Warsaw Jews in Walled Ghetto" discussed how Hitler had segregated thirty-eight thousand Jews in that city. German newspapers were shown to be bragging that Warsaw would have no Jewish businesses outside the ghetto walls.[171] As the war dragged into the winter, new wrinkles emerged, as Italy invaded Greece[172] and Hitler sought an alliance with the Soviet Union.[173]

In Honolulu, Harry relished the island weather during his first Christmas away from home. Despite ten inches of snow and record subzero temperatures inundating Chippewa Falls, ranging from −20 and −38 degrees Fahrenheit,[174] followed up days later by a ten-inch snowstorm that slowed Chippewa Falls to a standstill, Harry remained nostalgic for the family and good food back home.[175]

Dear Mother,

I got your card…also the one from Robert and Marie.

I'm sitting up late tonight getting out Christmas cards. I've had to stay aboard a lot lately for fire watches. It is hard to believe that Christmas is here because I'm on the ship so much.…There is no snow or cold weather.

How I wish I could spend the holidays with you and get some of your good home-cooked meals. Remember how I'd refuse to eat pineapple? Boy… now I go crazy. I guess Hawaii and the Dole Pineapple Company did that to me. We'll have a nice dinner on Christmas Day but I still would prefer some home-cooked chicken.

Don't feel disappointed about not sending a present because I have everything I need. Boy oh boy those eats will make up for that. My appetite

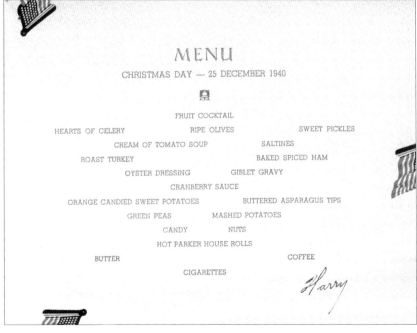

Christmas menu from the USS *California*, 1940. *Author's collection.*

is something I still carry with me. Whenever I go to Washington I order a
nice big waffle with syrup and butter…mmm.
　　　I heard that when we come back…we might stay for five or six months.
Maybe a chance to come back home—I hope.
　　　Merry Christmas and love to all,
　　　Harry

———

Letter No. 20: Eva and Ralph Kramer to their son Harry
December 25, 1940—Christmas Day
From: Chippewa Falls, WI
To: USS California

With reelection secured, Roosevelt entered the holiday season with more
political freedom to make the hard decisions. One of the first items on
his agenda was the creation of a four-man board to coordinate America's
national defense buildup. Roosevelt envisioned the board as a centralized
authority that could oversee every aspect of the war production process,
including labor, management and the overall product supply chain, from
buyer to user.

　　　Roosevelt also announced that Britain would be renegotiating its war
material contracts, as the embattled nation sought an additional $3 billion in
supplies, including sixty merchant ships paid for in cash.[176] The administration
warned, however, that no contracts would be signed until Congress passed
the president's "lend-lease" program. Across the country, hundreds of U.S.
companies signed contracts to produce items for the War Department. In
Harry's hometown, the Chippewa Falls Woolen Mill received its fifth of the
year, another $48,000 for overcoats,[177] while the Chippewa Glove Company
secured a $94,000 contract for ninety thousand pairs of leather gloves.[178]

　　　In Europe, Germany and Great Britain recognized a Christmas truce, just
days after Nazi air raids terrorized residents in Manchester, Liverpool and
London. During his Christmas address, Roosevelt verbalized the suffering
in Britain by explaining, "Most human beings want a peaceful chance" to
"better the world in a voluntary way," not in a manner "imposed on the
world by conquest."[179]

　　　In Chippewa Falls, the Kramers tried to enjoy the holiday season.
Eva and Ralph had never celebrated Christmas without Harry, and his
absence left a noticeable sadness. On Christmas morning, Eva sat down

at the kitchen table and wrote a heartfelt letter to her youngest son. She talked about spending the holiday with Robert, his wife, Marie, and their four sons. Earl was the most recent addition, born in November. She also acknowledged the frugality of the holiday, as a reduction in Ralph's salary had left them scraping. Despite the hardships, Eva made it known that the family still made do and had as enjoyable and memorable a Christmas as they could, considering.[180]

> *Dear, dear Harry,*
>
> *The lovely Christmas card and dear letter came…just in time to make us very happy on Christmas. It was appreciated because we hadn't expected to hear from you again for some time. You see we had received a card and a message from Ruth Liddiard* [Harry's first cousin once removed] *that they had heard "the California had left Bremerton for paths unknown." Now that we know you will be there till the 26th as planned we feel better. We went over to your brother's house to see the children get their Christmas things…trucks, books, animals, etc.*
>
> *David got a doll dressed in red…talked to it like last year…got into Dad's chair and rocked it. He is a cute baby…talks a lot now. Baby Earl got many gifts. Carl gave me something he made at school. Two paper plates…to form a pocket for holding letters. The Grip family* [Harry's sister-in-law Marie's parents] *were pleased with their gifts…coconut novelties, and asked me to thank you. Mrs. Grip said, "I'd like to write to Harry if I ever get time." She certainly does work hard. Mr. Grip has been painting in Eau Claire so that leaves the chores for her.*
>
> *They gave us a chicken.…How we wish you were here to help us eat it. Just Grandma Ualia, Dad, and I here alone. But we will plan many dinners when you come home. Won't that be grand if you get leave in March? We won't plan too strongly…just hope and pray you can.*
>
> [Harry's great-aunt] *Eva Bartingale sent a box of eats, including apples, oranges, nuts, candy, raisins, etc. We'll save some of the nuts for you. I hope our box of things were not too dry. I know the penuche wasn't so good. I would have made another batch, only I didn't have time.*
>
> *Both Ruth and Great Aunt Minnie praised you…said the boys were proud to call you cousin. It did my heart good.*
>
> *On account of dad's cut in wages we couldn't do much. Dad gave me stockings and I gave him a couple of ties which he bought himself, ha! I enjoyed wrapping the things you sent. Thank you for the lovely towel and all the loving thoughtfulness that came with it. Grandma Ualia liked her*

pin, but Dad thought she would just roll up the wall hanging and put it away, so he is going to hang it at the foot of the stairs where all can enjoy. She likes the flower holders so if it isn't too much trouble when you go back and aren't too expensive you might bring her one. I'll pay for it. Now that we all have something from Hawaii, don't spend any more money on us.

Your friend Mort Anderson liked his sport shirt. He felt bad he couldn't send you something but we couldn't tell him what you wanted. You will have to send us a list of the things you can have or need, then we'll know what to send. I suppose eats will head the list. Yes, I do remember how you disliked pineapple when I tried to fool you and put it in the Jell-O. I'm glad you like it now. The meals must get monotonous on ships so it is nice you can get off and get some special treat.

Jessie and Ralph Selden just called and said you had had an awful storm along the coast. I hope there wasn't much damage done and that you are alright. We haven't had our radio on much…so didn't hear of it. Jessie said Jack just loves his shirt and will write to you soon. You probably got their card.

Well, I guess that's all I can think of just now so I will say good night…Happy New Year with all the good things I know you have earned.

Lovingly,

Mother and Dad

Chapter 2

1941: "THE THINGS WE HAVE TO BE THANKFUL FOR"

Letter No. 21: Harry Kramer to his friend Jack Selden
January 17, 1941
From: Long Beach, CA
To: Chippewa Falls, WI

Any hope that a new year might lessen global hostilities quickly dissipated. Shortly after the two-day Christmas truce, bombings resumed between Great Britain and Germany. Since November, Nazi air raiders had carried out 80 major attacks and 325 smaller ones. Germany estimated that they dropped nearly one hundred million pounds of bombs on Britain, constituting a staggering twenty-five to one pound-per-pound advantage for Germany. Unfortunately for Hitler, Italy's offensive push into Greece left Mussolini reeling, as the country suffered major losses and setbacks along the way. On January 2, a disgruntled Hitler sent warplanes to bolster Mussolini's wobbling forces.[181]

Sensing Great Britain wouldn't make it through the year, Roosevelt pushed for Congress to pass a lend-lease program to give Britain more weapons without immediate cash payment. With the inauguration days away, the president felt confident his proposal would pass, as the Democratic Party controlled large majorities in both chambers of Congress.[182] Many high-profile Republicans were also supportive, including recently defeated Wendell Willkie. Willkie agreed that if Great Britain collapsed, the "free way of life" would pass from America as well.[183] Passage of a final bill was likely two months away.

In the interim, the Roosevelt administration predicted military defense costs would double by the end of the year.[184] Roosevelt and Congress had already doubled the size of the U.S. Army, from three hundred thousand to six hundred thousand, but they wanted more. New tanks, rifles, motor vehicles, arms and supplies and warplanes had increased at similar rates, with much more on the way. Roosevelt wanted most aspects of the army doubled by the end of 1941.[185]

The U.S. Navy had also increased, from 158,000 to 250,000. Not satisfied, the administration announced it would be reorganizing the two-ocean fleet into three in a military directive known as General Order 143: Organization Forces of the Naval Forces of the United States. The roster of 321 combat-ready ships, which would soon be infused with forty-two thousand additional men, would be allocated into three fleets: the Atlantic, Pacific and Asiatic Fleets.[186] To fund this, Roosevelt and Congress were contemplating a series of record income tax hikes.[187]

When discussing America's military buildup, the secretary of the navy, Frank Knox, warned the American people that it was not nearly enough. He speculated that the navy would likely commission 100 new ships within the next two years but that the Axis powers would construct 304 during the same window. The Axis powers already had an estimated 658 ships at sea, double what the United States had. In particular, the Axis powers maintained a glaring advantage in the number of submarines, cruisers and destroyers. The two naval areas where the United States lagged, albeit not by much, was in aircraft carriers (six to the Axis powers' eight) and battleships (fifteen to the Axis's twenty).[188] Knox bluntly assessed that the United States desperately needed more "time," as estimates predicted it would take six years to outfit a three-fleet navy. Knox surmised, "Only Britain and its fleet can give us that time. And they need our help to survive."[189]

The Japanese press continued to lash out over America's military buildup. When the secretary of state, Cordell Hull, warned a House committee that Axis control of the high seas would prove problematic, the Japanese press labeled him as symbolic of America's "pigheaded" and "anti-Japanese" views. Hull's comments were labeled as being rooted in "malice and hatred" for Japan and constituted a "clear challenge to the Axis Powers short of an ultimatum."[190]

With tensions simmering, Harry and the *California* started the new year sailing to California. During his liberty time, Harry visited with distant relatives from his mom's side of the family. Minerva "Minnie" Durfee, seventy-nine, was Eva's aunt. Born in Chippewa Falls, the widowed "Great

Harry about to take his first airplane ride in San Diego, California, 1940. *Author's collection.*

Aunt Minnie" raised her two surviving children, Ruth Liddiard and Morien Eugene Durfee Sr., in Washington State. The family relocated to California, where Morien Sr. would make a name for himself as a famous and successful architect. His California work included the Kraemer Building in Anaheim and the Chapman Building in Fullerton.[191]

In this letter, Harry ecstatically shared that he had taken his first airplane ride. It was something he had always dreamed of doing. His second cousin Glen Liddiard, Ruth's son, flew the two men high above the city of San Diego.

Harry also informed Jack about an amusement park in Long Beach called the Pike. Founded in 1902 along the city's shoreline, the Pike was known for having "independent arcades, food stands, gift shops, fair-style rides, a large bathhouse, and a municipal pier" that extended into the ocean. For Harry, it reminded him of the lighted midway at the annual Northern Wisconsin State Fair in Chippewa Falls.[192] The Pike would remain a cultural mainstay of Long Beach until its closure in 1979.[193]

> *Dear Jack,*
> *I was happy to read about dear old Wisconsin. I often think of being home…playing around in those snow drifts. The climate is wonderful in California but I still miss winter. In place of ice-skating I substitute bowling now…Enjoy it a lot.*

Harry and his second
cousin Glen Liddiard,
1940. *Author's collection.*

You'd guess, by the way I've not answered your letters that I'd gone to China....I'll try being more prompt. While in Bremerton...every day or most of the time at night I would have to stand a fire watch. There wasn't much to do....Got rather monotonous just standing by an electric welder with a fire extinguisher for six hours. On my liberties I always go to Seattle and stay overnight at the "Y." The ferry is the only way of traveling there and all the sailors start singing "I Love to Ride the Ferry."

Before my last trip to Washington, while at Long Beach, I got my first leave of seven days and...never forget the wonderful times I had. I spent my week in La Jolla—near San Diego—at my Great Aunt Minnie's. I met my cousins for the first time and they showed me a swell vacation. They are about my age and two of them have cars so each night...we'd pile in one of the cars and go out to enjoy ourselves. We'd first take in the best miniature golf course in San Diego followed by a show at a nifty drive-in. Glen Liddiard [Harry's second cousin] *has a pilot's license....He took me up for my first airplane ride. We went high over San Diego and he pointed out different places to me. Boy oh boy it was really swell and something to remember.*

The Pike in Long Beach, California, reminded Harry of the Northern
Wisconsin State Fair in Chippewa Falls, Wisconsin, circa 1940. *Author's collection.*

We have been out to sea for gunnery but…plan to go over to see the Durfee Family before we shove off. These people are also relatives…I visit them every time we come in. Gene Durfee [Harry's second cousin] *works at the Douglas Aircraft Plant in Santa Monica so I haven't spent time with him much. He wants to go to Los Angeles and see Artie Shaw and his orchestra.*

You know our fair back home with all the rides, games, stands, etc.? Well the Pike is just like that year around. The waterfront consists of stands, rides, etc. just like our fairs without a grandstand and racetrack. At night the place is crowded with sailors. There is a swell theater on the Pike with a big double feature bill plus a very good vaudeville show for 20 cents.

I'm sure you enjoy your Winchester and practice quite a bit. If I ever get leave we'll go big "game hunting"! I knew it was out of season to give you that shirt but am glad you like it. I have one myself and plan to try it out when it warms up.

Regards to all,
Harry

P.S. I forgot to thank you for that swell snapshot…and birthday and Christmas cards.

———

Letter No. 22: Eva Kramer to her son Harry Kramer
February 10, 1941
From: Chippewa Falls, WI
To: USS California

On January 20, 1940, fifty-eight-year-old Franklin Roosevelt became the only American president to take the oath of office for a third time. The weather in D.C. was twenty-nine degrees Fahrenheit, with sunny skies and a brisk wind.[194] Speaking from the east portico of the Capitol, Roosevelt gave a seventeen-minute speech highlighting America's obligation to other democracies. He explained, "There are men who doubt this. There are men who believe democracy…is limited…[and] that for some unexplained reason, tyranny and slavery have become the surging wave of the future— and that freedom is an ebbing tide.…In the face of great perils never before encountered," Roosevelt concluded, "our strong purpose is to protect and to perpetuate the integrity of democracy."[195]

Within days of his speech, Republican opposition to the lend-lease proposal began to surface, including that of U.S. Senator Alexander Wiley of Wisconsin. The Chippewa Falls native supported the concept, in principle, but stated that the current bill was not something he could support. Wiley warned that the Congress would be abdicating too much of its authority to Roosevelt during a time of peace, which constituted an "extreme centralization of power" to the executive branch.[196]

One of the most notable and vocal opponents of the lend-lease proposal was America First's Charles Lindbergh. Testifying before the House Foreign Affairs Committee, he argued that aiding Britain "was a mistake" and that the amount supplied by the United States was "not going to be sufficient." Instead, Lindbergh called for Congress and Roosevelt to invest in a string of air bases around the country and to create a national air force with ten thousand first-line planes, with an additional ten thousand in reserve. "This," he argued, was the best way to "ensure American security." The outspoken Lindbergh went a step further by asserting that

Group photo of the USS *California*'s officers and enlisted men, 1940. Harry has been circled in white. *U.S. Navy.*

Britain and the United States were incapable of winning the war "on the present basis" and urged all involved to seek a "negotiated peace" with the Axis powers. "I think it would be impossible that England and the United States could invade the continent together" unless an internal "collapse" came from within Germany or Italy.[197] In response to Lindbergh, the U.S. ambassador to France, William Bullitt, warned the committee, "If the British Navy were destroyed…invasion of the western hemisphere would be almost certain."[198]

Further complicating the lend-lease bill were warnings issued by Axis leaders and surrogates. Mussolini's spokesperson warned that the bill violated the United States' neutrality and predicted "some unforeseen and quite unpleasant reaction at the end of their path."[199] Hitler went further by stating, "Germany has no quarrel with the American people." But, he declared, "If non-European powers try to intervene here…every ship that comes within reach…will be torpedoed."[200] On February 9, the House of Representatives passed the Lend-Lease Act by a largely partisan vote of 260 to 165. It would take another month before a Senate vote.[201]

The day after the House passed the bill, Eva sat down and wrote a letter to Harry. She let him know that the package he mailed from Bremerton had arrived, which included a fake newspaper story featuring Harry. He also mailed home an 8″ x 10″ photo showing the *California*'s entire complement of crew and officers, with himself marked in the photo so they could find him.[202]

Dear Harry,

A package of old letters came…to make room for more, I take it. Not knowing what was in the package I opened it and took out that newspaper on top, unfolded it and read—"Harry Kramer visits Waikīkī." Then began scanning to see what you had done to get your name in the paper. It finally dawned on me that it was a joke….We had a good laugh.

Your friend Mort Anderson came in after the box arrived and I said to him, "Did you know that Harry got his name in the paper?" He said, "No, what does it say?" When I showed him the paper he just hollered and said, "Well, for crying out loud." I'll bet you had a good chuckle when you packed them, thinking of the surprise in store for us. It certainly is a clever idea. The picture of the ship is sure grand—gives one an idea of the immensity of the ship and crew.

I looked for you among the tall ones, then among the officers, ha, ha! It was only after I got the magnifying glass that I saw the arrow pointing to your dear face. It's good considering the large group. I am still wondering how the boys got up on those guns. Dad took it down to be framed as it cracked in the mail.

Aunt Lizzie Budge spent a day with us last week—said she got your Christmas card and would like to write to you but her eyes are not very good and her hands are crippled from rheumatism. She thinks so much of you. I'm glad you remembered her with a card.

A week ago Sunday we went out to your brother Robert's house to see how the kiddies were after their sick spell, and I must tell you of the cute thing David did. Marie put him to bed thinking he'd go right to sleep, then went upstairs. David got out of bed, got a knife, climbed up on the cupboard and started sawing on a fresh cake Marie made. He is like his Uncle Harry, he likes cake. Marie says he is into everything. The baby lost weight when he was sick but is alright now.

Great Aunt Minnie Durfee wrote about her birthday party....I'll send the letter to you as it is so interesting.

Dad has been having a cold the past few days but has worked right along. His work is nearly through but I tell him not to worry. We have been wonderfully cared for.

I thought the enclosed clipping was good and you could use it for your scrapbook.

Lots of love from us all,
Mother

Letter No. 23: Eva Kramer to her son Harry Kramer
February 14, 1941
From: Chippewa Falls, WI
To: USS California

Momentum continued to build on Capitol Hill for Roosevelt's Lend-Lease Act. On February 11, Wendell Willkie testified in favor of the bill before the Senate's Foreign Relations Committee. Agreeing with Roosevelt that the British needed both "immediate" and "long term" assistance, Willkie warned that if Britain fell, it would likely lead to Nazi aggression against America. Having sensed that Republican senators were fearful of giving Roosevelt too much power, Willkie encouraged them to include "all modifications" deemed appropriate in order to limit "any unnecessary authority." He suggested they could meet the president "halfway" by passing the bill with tangible limits, such as confining the aid to only Britain, China and Greece. Willkie made it clear that he supported the program due to his "great desire for national unity."[203]

Alexander Wiley remained skeptical. He called for a closed executive session with Secretary of State Cordell Hull, in order to get a "realistic appraisal of American-British relations." He wanted to know what the administration knew regarding the coordination efforts of Germany, Italy and Japan. "If this situation is as grave as we might be led to believe it is," Wiley remarked, "then it is all-important for us to know the facts in contemplation of the lend-lease bill." Regardless of his concerns, the bill passed committee with a fifteen to eight vote, with a full Senate vote coming soon.[204]

Two days later, Secretary Hull confirmed to the press that an urgent, yet precautionary, message from the State Department had instructed Americans to withdraw from countries in the Far East, especially China and Japan. This action coincided with an Australian government statement that "the war has moved into a new stage involving the utmost gravity," as intelligence suggested Japan was poised to move against British or Dutch possessions in the Far East.[205]

On Valentine's Day, Eva found herself missing her son more than usual. In this letter, Eva covered many topics, including Harry's inquiry into the draft status of his classmates. Twenty-one-year-old Benjamin Smith, who lived at 28 Maple Street, on the city's south side, was heading off to Fort Sheridan, Illinois.[206] Twenty-year-old Loyal Lubach, who lived near Harry at 20 Division Street, was still four months away from his twenty-first birthday and not eligible to register. Harry's good friend Mort Anderson decided to enlist in the U.S. Army's Air Corps rather than wait to be drafted. By February 18, he had arrived in St. Louis, Missouri, for training.[207]

One by one, Eva witnessed several of Harry's friends drawn into the nation's peacetime draft. Despite all the world's challenges, Eva remained hopeful, stating, "If giving our boys for a little while will help then we must all do our bit cheerfully." But she did allow herself a moment to show both concern and confusion regarding it all by lamenting, "Only I cannot see how going over there will help unless we are attacked here."[208]

> *Dear Harry,*
> *If you only knew how much joy your letters bring! So glad to hear that you made the grade. We knew you would, and I do hope your new work will be interesting and instructive.*

I knew you would feel badly to hear that Mort had joined up. I've been hoping all along that you would get your leave before that happened. But as you say, he undoubtedly would have been called before long as he has no dependents and that is why he enlisted in the "Air Corps." He tried for the Navy awhile back but didn't make it—and like you, made up his mind suddenly. He stuck his head in the door one Monday night and said, "I passed and it won't be long now." We expected he'd come back to say goodbye but Mort said he went that night. It's just as well though, as it is hard to say goodbye. We do miss him running in and doing errands for us, easing the hurt of your going.

There are many sad changes in life and the draft is one of them. But we mustn't complain when we know of what poor mothers and fathers overseas are going through. If giving our boys for a little while will help then we must all do our bit cheerfully. Only I cannot see how going over there will help unless we are attacked here. And we must pray that something will turn evil aside. "God is everywhere and nothing unlike Him is present or has power." I have thought of these words a great deal lately and it has helped calm fears of a near conflict. I suppose it is uncertain about getting leave on account of the tension of things now, but maybe you and Mort could be home at the same time.

I am sure Mort will be tickled to get a letter from you as he must be lonely among strangers, and he has always been so free to come and go as he pleased, then to be plunged into routine and hardships is tough, but you've never complained.

Dad went over to Anderson's last night and got Mort's address and we were going to send it to you and write to him too. I'm glad you got a scrapbook. It will be interesting to read later on and nice for you to have all your life. I know you have a lot of fun making them too. Yes, I thought that cartoon was funny and so true. The recruiting officers make you think it is "going to be a picnic."

Benny Smith was in yesterday and I showed him the sailor picture you took of yourself, as well as the picture of the ship. He thought they were nice. We liked the postcards in your letter today as they do give one an idea of things as they are in the docks. You asked about Loyal Lubach, yes, he is still working at the store part-time, but his mother says he gets the urge to go west or join the Navy. He did work at the Chippewa Woolen Mill for a while, as did Mort, but they got laid off. I suppose Loyal will have to register for the draft this summer when he turns twenty-one.

Have been experiencing some very severe cold weather. 22° below zero and stayed around that for several days with a stiff wind blowing so we had to do some fires to keep the house warm. It is growing warmer tonight and we are glad. It's a good thing Dad had a few days off this week to bring in wood and carry out ashes. Yes, I too wish there was some job for dad. I try to know there is something that he can do, and don't worry about it. So perhaps it will work out alright.

Grandma Ualia was pleased to be remembered. She hasn't been feeling so good lately…has a cold. She doesn't often get sick. I hope you keep well dear boy and may God guide you and help you in your work.

Lots of love from us all,
Mother

P.S. We'll be looking for more of those good letters whenever you have time to write. Tell us about your new work.

———

Letter No. 24: Harry Kramer to his friend Jack Selden
February 19, 1941
From: Bremerton, WA
To: Chippewa Falls, WI

In the early months of 1941, Italy continued to struggle in Greece. In North Africa, British and German soldiers engaged for the first time.[209] On February 17, a newly signed nonaggression pact between Turkey and Bulgaria removed a major obstacle in Hitler's desire to send troops to the Mediterranean Sea. Hitler had hoped to keep Turkey on the sidelines, while the British sought to have Turkey enter as an ally. Turkey now "pledged to not fight if the Nazis entered Bulgaria," which severely reduced British influence in the Balkan region.[210] Days later, Hitler threatened Greece to either surrender now or run the risk of Germany adding sixty thousand Nazi reinforcements to Italy's ranks. Undeterred, Greece resisted.[211]

In Washington, D.C., the House of Representatives tentatively approved the development of Guam and Samoa as "naval aviation outposts," as part of a $242 million naval base development bill. Much had changed since Congress snubbed the idea a year ago, as Roosevelt kept the pressure on for naval upgrades. Despite Congress's fears that America's recent moves would amplify tensions with Japan, navy admiral Harold R. Stark alleviated their concerns. "Policy on defense works should not be dictated by any foreign power," Stark argued. "Any protest from Japan on that score should be totally disregarded."[212]

It had been a month since Harry had written to his friend Jack Selden. The *California* had sailed back to Bremerton, Washington, from a short stay in California. Harry shared that he passed a recent naval exam, earning him a promotion from fireman third class to fireman second class. This also ensured him a modest pay increase, which Harry responsibly sent home to be saved for post-navy life. Knowing his parents' fragile financial situation, the dutiful son made it known they could access the account whenever needed.

Harry also talked about his affinity for music. He preferred more traditional jazz artists, consisting of a big band using an assortment of saxophones, trumpets and trombones, which were often accompanied by a piano, clarinet, violin and singers. He began purchasing records of songs by his favorite musicians, including those by Hal Kemp and Kay Kyser. Differing from many his age, Harry was not much interested in the growing wave of jitterbug-style jazz. The fast-paced music, often called jive or jump, was often blended with energetic and acrobatic ballroom and swing dances such as the Jitterbug or the Lindy Hop.[213] Harry maintained more traditional tastes.

While docked in Bremerton, Harry spent his liberty enjoying a variety of offerings at the Craven Center, an entertainment center for servicemen at the corner of Burwell Street and Park Avenue. The venue provided a convenient, affordable and respectable environment for sailors to let loose, without succumbing to the temptations of vice or other unsavory offerings. One of the hit movies Harry viewed here was *You'll Find Out*, a comedic horror film mixed with musical numbers starring Kay Kyser. In the film, Kyser and his band go to a "spooky and desolate house" and are trapped there after a bridge goes out. The band's "young hostess confides that someone has been trying to kill her," and Kyser and his bandmates solve the mystery.[214]

Outside the structured confines of the Craven Center, however, was a world of new experiences that not every sailor was socially or financially equipped to effectively manage. Harry alluded to one who spent his money as fast as he could earn it, presumably on partying and drinking. By contrast, the introspective Harry had recently become interested in scrapbooking, so he could document his life in the navy, as well as his love of airplanes, movies and comical cartoons.[215]

Dear Jack,
You should see how everyone drops his work and runs to mail call. And the person who walks away with the most sure feels proud. I got two myself.

Liberty began at 12:45 so I dressed and hurried for that gangway. Most of this afternoon I've been at Craven Center. It is a gathering place, like a YMCA, for all the men of the service and one may do almost anything to pass the time. There are bowling alleys, pool tables, and a library. Every other night there is a free show….Just saw one called "Too Many Girls." I don't know if I'd agree with the title!!! It was one of those musicals, with plenty of songs and dancing. Last week Kay Kyser and his band played in the movie "You'll Find Out." Boy did he play swell popular songs. Being down in the fresh water hold all day, I miss out on having a radio so I go for music when I get a chance. I never did like this jitterbug stuff, but love to hear the popular orchestras play songs like "It All Comes Back to Me Now." One of my hobbies, when in Long Beach, is to get a record of my favorite tune. I have some down at my cousin's place in La Jolla, as there isn't a place on board to keep anything.

You must be learning a lot about radio as you spoke of going for a license. That's a good thing….Keep it up. That's one advantage you have on the outside of being able to set up a workshop in your room. I've found one thing I'm enjoying…making scrapbooks. I bought a nice one at the stationery store, and been keeping my scissors busy, cutting out prize navy cartoons and articles to fill its pages. I start chuckling to myself as my eyes wander over the comical pictures. There are many serious items in it too. I'm starting a department for airplanes and one for movies. Some of the other boys would do things like that but the majority sit around and talk about how much they drink.

I suppose you know about Mort Anderson leaving. It was a surprise to me. If I was home it would seem strange not having him drop in everyday like he did.

Out in the main room, I noticed that there are ice skating parties at the ice bowl. It would be fun to try it again so next time my liberty starts I'm going to take a bus and go out.

The day before yesterday the log room published the list of all the men who made their rates, showing the exams of a month ago. I was happy to find my name there so now I have another white stripe added to my cuff on the dress blue jumper and am in the $54 [monthly] *pay grade. I'm going to make out another allotment as that is the best way to save money, having it sent home directly from Washington each month. So many of the men get payed off at the end of the four year enlistment with only their last month's pay to their name. One boy in our division went over to Long Beach and Los Angeles with $103.00 in his pocket and came back with* *enough to buy a 3 cent stamp. I don't know how he spent so much but I surely could have had a good time for a fraction of that amount.*

Is it very cold there? The weather is nice most of the time here except for occasional fog. Today I came over without a coat and it was warm in the afternoon.

Pardon the writing but I left my fountain pen on board and used one of the drip pens on the desk here.

Give my regards to all,

Harry (make the gangway) Kramer

———

Letter No. 25: Harry Kramer to his mother, Eva Kramer
April 20, 1941
From: Pearl Harbor, Honolulu, HI
To: Chippewa Falls, WI

Within the two-month span separating Harry's last letters, Congress passed historic legislation that would drastically alter the scale and scope of U.S. foreign policy for decades. On March 8, the Senate overwhelmingly passed Roosevelt's Lend-Lease Act by a margin of 60–31. The new law allowed the administration to distribute "large quantities of food and war materials" to Great Britain, including "tanks, aircraft, ships, weapons, and road building supplies…clothing, chemicals and food." This would allow the United States to engage the Axis powers without entering the war. Days later, the Senate passed legislation to develop naval bases on the Pacific Islands of Guam and Samoa, as well as to upgrade newly acquired British holdings in the Atlantic.[216] Roosevelt signed both into law and immediately asked Congress to pass a record $7 billion in aid through the program.[217]

Senators opposed to the Lend-Lease Act included both Wisconsin senators, Alexander Wiley and Robert La Follette Jr., the son of legendary politician Robert "Fighting Bob" La Follette. Wiley predicted the bill would allow Hitler to "goad Japan into attacking the United States." "Under ordinary circumstances," Wiley surmised, "it would mean war." He argued that ultimately, it depended on how the Axis powers viewed the legislation, but that the law abdicated congressional authority by pre-authorizing Roosevelt to "intervene."[218]

Although they were expensive for a sailor to purchase, Shavemaster electric razors were a popular luxury onboard the USS *California*, circa 1940. *Author's collection.*

Overseas, Axis leaders planned to meet to discuss their response to the Lend-Lease Act. Sources in Italy speculated "an impending Japanese move under the triple alliance." The Italian newspaper *La Tribuna* bluntly declared, "Yesterday America spoke. Soon Japan will say its word." Unfazed by the journalistic rhetoric, the United States continued plans to deliver the first twenty thousand planes to Great Britain while securing an airfield-sharing pact with Mexico. Roosevelt wanted options to defend the Panama Canal.[219] While Germany expanded military activity into Greenland, Northern Ireland, Yugoslavia, Bulgaria and Greece, Roosevelt warned that the American people were not yet adequately aware of the "acuteness of the war situation in Europe" but were becoming increasingly aware as each day passed.[220]

The *California*, meanwhile, returned to Hawaii after spending four months in Washington and California. Just prior to their return, Harry and the crew briefly docked near San Francisco. Luckily, it was Harry's turn to take liberty; he marveled at the Golden Gate Bridge and took a long walk down the city's famed Market Street district. While perusing the various shops, Harry purchased himself a Sunbeam Shavemaster Men's Electric Razor. Although the innovative electric razors had become popular among military servicemen, they were also expensive. Williams Brothers Company, located at 426 Market Street, was a cutlery and specialty item shop that sold Shavemaster razors for $15.75,[221] or roughly $277.00 today.[222] Harry assured his mother that he had already tried one out and that the purchase was a functional one. The ever-mindful son worried about the perceived extravagance of the purchase.

By late April, Harry and the *California* had returned to Pearl Harbor Naval Station. On board the ship was Walter Davenport, a journalist from *Collier's* magazine. The navy had been searching for a "first rate reporter" who would publish "at least one true story" regarding the Pacific Fleet. Accordingly, *Collier's* accepted the navy's request and dispatched Davenport for three weeks aboard *California*. His immersion culminated with the article, "Impregnable Pearl Harbor," published in the June 14 edition. Davenport confidently observed, "Our Navy [is] visibly ready for anything in the Pacific." He added, "You've got to be pretty pessimistic to visualize any invader establishing himself on the island of Oahu, the fortress of the Hawaiian Archipelago," referring to Oahu's isolation and the military presence there.[223]

Although Harry relished the excitement of Davenport's presence on the ship, it was his return to Waikiki Beach that he was most eager for.[224]

Dear Mother,

There is about 4,000 miles plus separating us again. I didn't know at the time I sent my last letter from Bremerton that we were headed this way but I might have guessed it. You got my card from San Francisco, I suppose. The ship anchored there just overnight but I happened to rate liberty that day and got off the gangway right after supper. It was a big thrill to see that famous bridge for the first time and so close at hand. Our liberty boat passed beneath it on the way to the dock and the cars looked like tiny toys. It was so high. After landing most of us stopped into the big Army-Navy YMCA. Then later I traveled up San Francisco's Market Street and it was long—wow! I walked a mile or so before I even caught a glimpse of the main part of it including the theaters, etc. There are some huge stores there which have swell window designs. I was sorry to go back so soon and leave but it couldn't be helped. Ever since that day we left, our bow was pointed southward for 2,200 miles, and old Pearl Harbor came into view.

This makes the third time I've been to the islands now and I can't say I hate the liberty here. In fact, I love it but must be careful not to say that in front of my shipmates as they'd think I was nuts. You see most of them don't like it, being married and away from their families in the States. Some

Harry poses, in his navy whites, on Honolulu's famous Waikiki Beach, 1940. The Royal Hawaiian Hotel can be seen over his left shoulder. *Author's collection.*

of the other ships have been out here steady for nearly a year except when they go back for a week or two every third or fourth month.

Yesterday and today, I tucked my swimming suit under my arm and bee-lined for Waikīkī Beach. I've been reclining peacefully on the sands of Oahu, along with the millionaires of the Royal Hawaiian Hotel (they must be at $25.00 a day) and letting old Sol put his best coat of brown on me. I don't rate liberty now until Wednesday but I'll be back again. Another boy and I are going to take a trip to the other side of the island and go swimming there. He has a portable radio which is carried on a shoulder strap. Lying on the soft sand in the warm sun with swing music—ah—it's perfect!

Walter Davenport, the well-known writer for Collier's magazine, came over on the USS California and is staying with us for a month. I see him quite often as I'm in the log room and go back to the officer's area every few minutes for something or other. He is getting material about the Navy for a future series of articles for Colliers.

I haven't added that extra amount to my allotment yet as I'm buying a few extra things that I've wanted. I got myself a new electric razor. It is a Shavemaster and sure works well. My face was getting so painful from using safety razors that I thought it best to get it. Another boy let me use his a few times before I bought my own so I knew how it was going to work.

I hope Dad is feeling better since having trouble with his legs and hope everyone else is well too. I say Aloha to Grandma Ualia and Dad.

Lovingly,
Harry

Letter No. 26: Harry Kramer to his friend Jack Selden
May 13, 1941
From: Pearl Harbor, Honolulu, HI
To: Chippewa Falls, WI

By mid-May, the American military buildup showed formidable results. General George C. Marshall, the army's chief of staff, confidently reported that the country had "gotten over the hump." He added that the "army has the highest morale I've ever seen," and that the peacetime draft had expanded the ranks to 1.25 million men, up from 169,000 in just two years.[225] Impressed but not satisfied with domestic defense production, Roosevelt called on suppliers to work their machines "24 hours a day and seven days a week" to fill the demand for munitions, planes, ships and other supplies.[226] The Chippewa Shoe Company was one such company to plot aggressive expansion. It announced a one-third increase in domestic shoe production and prepared itself to meet any future war production orders. To secure enough manufacturing space, the company leased the top three floors of the Chippewa Glove Company building, located on the corner of Central and High Streets.[227]

The most glaring need, in Roosevelt's eyes, was the manufacturing of large and heavy long-range aerial bombers. The president called for a monthly goal of "500 long-range, four motor bombers" to be built—ten times the current pace. These aircraft, the president believed, would constitute an "offensive weapon which the Axis could not meet."[228] Unfortunately, these successes placed serious strain on the nation's finances. Commerce Secretary Jesse Jones forecasted the national debt would exceed $90 billion. In response, Congress began crafting historically high income-tax brackets to generate an immediate $3.6 billion in revenue. Workers in all tax brackets faced steep tax increases, with estimates ranging from two to six times more than what workers currently paid.[229]

Despite the tax increases, the American people remained firmly behind Roosevelt. A Gallup poll revealed a 73 percent job approval rating. Overall, the American people favored giving Great Britain war supplies but fervently opposed direct United States involvement; 69 percent were against sending U.S. pilots and sailors. Even though 82 percent believed the United States would eventually end up in the war at some point, a whopping 81 percent opposed entry at that time.[230]

Charles Lindbergh, who continued to predict that Germany could not be defeated, saw his public feud with Roosevelt escalate. Roosevelt compared the famed aviator to the "appeasers who urged peace" during the eras of the American Revolution and the Civil War. In response, Lindbergh resigned his position as a colonel in the United States Army Air Corps Reserve, a position that would turn active in the event of war.[231] When a reporter asked Roosevelt's press secretary, Stephen Early, about Lindberg's recent resignation, Early quipped, "Leads me to wonder if he is returning his decoration to Mr. Hitler," as well. Early was referring to an honorary medal, called the Service Cross of the German Eagle, given to Lindbergh on a visit to Germany. As for the commission Lindbergh gave up, Early bluntly stated, "The President indicated [Lindbergh] wouldn't have any duties if he continued to hold his commission. Now there is a commission someone else can have."[232]

With each passing day, Lindbergh's positions were becoming a liability, with only 24 percent approving and 63 percent opposing.[233] In late April, the *Chippewa-Herald Telegram* published a map showing the vast and ever-expanding lands held by the Axis powers. It was staggering. The headline read "Hitler Breaks Even with Napoleon on Conquests."[234] Within weeks, Hitler had expanded his ground troops east, into Greece, while simultaneously engaging in aerial bombings to the west, striking cities in Northern Ireland and Scotland.[235]

Hitler's Germany, however, did have setbacks. Winston Churchill had announced that his Royal Air Force bombing of key German cities had increased significantly—including the capital, Berlin—as the fruits of America's Lend-Lease Act became reality. Churchill confirmed that the recently acquired Douglas A-20 Havoc medium-range bombers had been instrumental in destroying German airfields in northern France and Belgium. These offensive air raids would prove instrumental in keeping the Luftwaffe's terror raids largely away from city of London.[236]

More embarrassing for Hitler was the personal and political fallout stemming from the bizarre actions of Rudolf Hess, one of his longest-serving and most loyal sycophants. In the early hours of Saturday, May 10, a lone German airman parachuted onto a farm in Scotland just moments before his plane crashed. The detained airman, who had just flown one thousand miles through a war zone, told the farmer he wanted to see the Duke of Hamilton, whom he believed would broker a peace between Great Britain and Germany, on terms advantageous to Hitler. The delusional pilot was none other than Rudolf Hess, the deputy führer of Nazi Germany and second in the line of succession to Hitler. Hess's erratic behavior appeared to be rooted in a desire to regain favor with Hitler. The two had once been close; Hess typed Hitler's memoir, *Mein Kampf*, while the two were in prison. But there was no peace deal as a result of Hess's stunt. The Nazi Party quickly dismissed Hess as a deranged man who was prone to "hallucinations" and "fateful delusion."[237]

In Hawaii, Harry wrote Jack Selden. In playful banter between friends, Harry opened his letter with war-related humor relating to the infrequency of his writing. It had been nearly two months since his last letter to Jack, so Harry informed him of his new assignment in the engine's log room.[238]

Dear Jack,
You must think I'm more than four thousand miles off by the way my letters have not arrived. Maybe I'd better start my own blitzkrieg—with paper.

Harry poses in front of the Royal Hawaiian Hotel on Waikiki Beach, 1940. *Author's collection.*

This is my third time here....Swimming is first on my list of pleasures. And the place—yes that's right "Waikīkī Beach." The more I go... the more I enjoy. Blue pacific sea, rolling surge, pure white sand, liquid sunshine, bright Hawaiian swimming trunks, sighing palm trees, and pretty girls!! How does that sound? A little out of the ordinary? It's just as good as it sounds. I think sailors enjoy these places more than civilians because when you come in from two or three weeks at sea, you really appreciate scenery again. Boy if I ever get to come home during your summer vacation prepare to go on some long hikes...or a camping trip.

School will soon be out? Boy how time flies. It seems but a few days ago I was sitting in the rear of the high school assembly. How much better do you like it than junior high?

Night before last on our quarterdeck a big hula show was held for the officers and crew of the USS California and USS New Mexico. There were two thousand sailors in all and everyone had fun. A professional troupe staged the show....They were really good. One of the hula girls who was exceptionally pretty would wander among the gold braid pick an ensign or higher officer and make him do a native dance before the crowd. It's comical to see your division officer waving his arms around trying in vain to do an imitation of a hula dance. The crowd yelled enough especially when the girl hung a beautiful flower lei around his neck and give him a kiss for his work.

I'm now working in the log room for this quarter. I take care of the division paper and record books. Sometimes it is a madhouse with all the officers wanting to know where so and so is or sending me with a message to some officer who is harder to locate than a needle in a haystack. However, just lately the M Division has taken over all the watches at sea, so I haven't so much to do then.

There is some kind of a performance about to start at the "Y" which warrants investigating. Say "Hello" to all the folks for me.

Aloha,

Harry

Letter No. 27: Harry Kramer to his mother, Eva Kramer
June 17, 1941
From: Pearl Harbor, Honolulu, HI
To: Chippewa Falls, WI

As spring gave way to summer, the Axis powers continued their advancements in Europe. The fall of the island of Crete and its alignment with the government of Vichy France had practically eliminated the Mediterranean Sea as an oil link between Great Britain and countries in the Middle East and North Africa. The Mediterranean was now an "Axis Sea." Hitler and Mussolini once again met at Brenner Pass to plot their next moves, as the British and their allies still firmly controlled the Suez Canal and the Middle East.[239] Hitler, still fuming about the irrational behavior of Rudolf Hess, was contemplating an invasion of Scotland in the West and a large mobilization against the Soviet Union in the East.[240]

With Germany boasting that Great Britain was "Bleeding to Death," due to the heavy losses inflicted on British merchant vessels, Roosevelt announced that "American ships will take over British routes" outside the war zone. These included those to Canada, Australia and New Zealand. The president had also recently severed relations with the Vichy government of France and took the unusual step of bypassing them in order to speak directly to the citizens of France. Roosevelt implored them to reject any "collaboration" of their government with a "military power whose central and fundamental policy calls for the utter destruction of freedom."[241] Weeks later, the Vichy government passed a law banning all Jews from participating in any "profession or business" and was contemplating a declaration of war against Britain.[242]

On Tuesday, May 27, Roosevelt gave a historic presidential address in which he declared that the country was in a "State of Unlimited Emergency." As a result, he would use "every means devised by military and naval experts" to defend America against attack or threat. He called on all citizens to develop a "united support against Hitlerism" and informed the citizenry that "your government has the right to expect all citizens to take part in the common work of our common defense." He warned the owners of factories, as well as their employed laborers, that any disputes would not be allowed to "interfere with war production" and ordered all work stoppages to be ceased. The "articles of defense," Roosevelt proclaimed, "must have the undisputed right of way in every industrial plant in the country." The president reaffirmed that the United States "will decide for ourselves whether and when, and where, our American interests are attacked or our security threatened."[243]

Shortly after a new government order to produce forty thousand military aircraft, striking workers formed a picket line in front of the factory gate of the North American Aviation Company in Inglewood, California.[244] Roosevelt responded swiftly and called on the striking workers to return to work by Monday or else he would take control of the factory. When Monday came, police officers were thwarted in their efforts to escort volunteering strike-breakers through the picket line. Roosevelt immediately authorized the United States Army to seize the plant, using three thousand armed soldiers, in order to allow workers to return. Within weeks, all the soldiers had left and a new contract had been agreed on by both ownership and labor.[245]

In response, Mussolini labeled Roosevelt "an authoritarian" and a future "dictator." He added that the United States was already in a "de-facto war" against the Axis powers and brushed off any concerns about the United States' future expansion into the conflict. "American intervention will not give Britain victory, only prolong [the war]," the Italian leader concluded. "They are too late."[246]

On June 8, an American merchant ship became the center of an international crisis. The SS *Robin Moor*, a commercial and passenger vessel sailing from New York to Cape Town, South Africa, was torpedoed and sunk by a German U-boat some 750 miles west of Sierra Leone.[247] The passengers and crew were initially feared dead, only to be discovered, by chance, floating in lifeboats. The Nazi sub commander had allowed them to disembark the vessel prior to his sinking of it. Rather than showing contrition, Germany declared that it was fully aware that the ship was American and pledged to sink more vessels if they were carrying "contraband" to any Great Britain–aligned locales.

In protest, Roosevelt announced that the United States would freeze all German and Italian financial assets, including those belonging to countries they were occupying.[248] Two days later, the president ordered the closure of all German consulates in the United States, citing activities that were "inimical to the welfare" of the United States. The administration did clarify, however, that these actions should not be viewed as a full break from diplomatic relations with Germany.[249]

In this letter to his mother, Harry alluded to the changes in global events. "There are a lot of things I'd like to write about," Harry wrote, "but have to be very careful and not divulge any information on the movements of ships, etc."[250] What Harry could reveal was that he was quickly rising up the ranks and was close to taking his fireman first class (F1C) exam. As a navy F1C, Harry would see his pay increase from fifty-four to sixty dollars a month.

Not only would passing the exam further enhance Harry's career and financial prospects in the navy, but the extra money would also go a long way toward helping sustain his family back home, as Harry learned that his father recently lost his latest job. As neither Harry's mom nor grandmother were employed outside of the home, Ralph's annual $612 salary, or $51 a month, was a necessity in preserving their livelihood at 21 Well Street.[251]

Despite the uncertainty surrounding his father's employment, Harry's prospects were on the rise. Harry informed his parents that he now worked in the ship's "machine shop." Harry liked working with his hands and was eager to do "lathe work" and craft whatever widgets were needed to maintain the vessel. It was a coveted position onboard *California*, and Harry was grateful for the opportunity. Although he did not elaborate, Harry acknowledged that he nearly got sent to the U.S. Navy's dirigible school in New Jersey. At the time, the navy had ten non-rigid airships, or blimps, which would inflate when filled with helium or hydrogen. One of their primary functions was to provide aerial reconnaissance by patrolling for submarines and other threats by sea.[252]

Compared to what Harry normally shared, he was quite candid about his life post–navy career. He envisioned owning a semi-secluded cabin, either in the "Canadian Rockies or around Yellowstone National Park," where he could "sing eight hours a day." Whether he was exaggerating or not, which he surely was, Harry's love of music was inseparable from the man.[253]

Prior to mailing, Harry added a paragraph that was directed to his father. In the June edition of the *National Geographic Magazine*, journalist F. Barrows Colton wrote an article called "Life in Our Fighting Fleet," which chronicled the life of sailors aboard ships in the Pacific Fleet. The thirty-one-page spread included thirty black-and-white photographs highlighting various scenes of navy life. One mouthwatering image showed two mess cooks laboring over a table of fourteen dessert pies with the caption: "Pie like mother used to make, and maybe even better!" Another photo showed six sailors eating dinner off cafeteria trays, with a caption including the navy slang for each food eaten: stew was "slum"; chicken or turkey, "seagull"; pancakes, "collision mats"; tomato catsup, "red lead"; and hash on toast, "mud on a shingle."[254] Harry thought his father would like to read it but made it clear that mom still made the best food.

> *Dear Mother,*
>
> *I feel guilty about my own correspondence as it's been several weeks. For the past month I've spent most all my spare moments studying for the coming examination. It is nice they let the messengers study on their night watches in the log room otherwise we'd just think about our bunks! I'm going for Fireman 1st Class and there are a lot of things to cover. Each of the three subjects for the test—engineering, math, and A to N— have a several hundred page book. The fireman's manual has practically got to be memorized….Been busy working on all fifteen chapters. If we pass…$60 a month is the pay grade for an F 1/C. I've heard them talking of a 10% increase for all enlisted personnel. Maybe it's a lot of scuttlebutt (bum dope)!*
>
> *There are things I'd like to write about but have to be very careful…not divulge information on the movements of ships, etc. I wish I knew when I could come home….Hard thing to count on in these times. I still have not heard from Mort Anderson…wondering if he'd be able to get home either. Gol darn—there's a beautiful Hawaiian song drifting over the air and I can hardly write. I'm just crazy about music and every place where there's*

a Sing Song in progress you'll find me in the crowd. I get an idea that when I retire I'll build myself a little cabin in the Canadian Rockies or around Yellowstone Park. Then sing eight hours a day. Gene Durfee wrote that he has his own apartment now and bought a $100 combination radio and phonograph. He has 200 records. It is also my ambition to collect my favorite pieces someday. The Liddiards have five of mine now.

Thanks Dad for your letter. I enjoy hearing about anything from Chippewa Falls. I'd enjoy getting back home in one of those good old thunderstorms or going on a hike up the river in a howling blizzard again. The kids can show me around and teach me all the things I forgot. I'm sorry about Dad having to lay off but we must know everything will come out alright. Next quarter I go to the machine shop for lathe work. It's pretty nice....Get a chance to learn machines down there. It is hard to get into the shop as a lot of the men come in from the many trade schools...but they were short a man and tried me out.

I almost got to go to Dirigible School in Lakehurst, New Jersey to study lighter than air work. They say its a swell shore station because you live in good barracks and can have civilian clothes when on liberty. The navy is building up her dirigible fleet as they are very important in patrol work. I'm always interested in aircraft and crane my head skyward to watch the dive bombers work out. Will be more prompt in the near future.

Love to all the family,

Harry

P.S. I want Dad to see the June issue of National Geographic Magazine. There is a big article about the fleet. Don't believe...about the chow as they don't make it as good as mother's meals, and I ought to know.

Letter No. 28: Harry Kramer to his mother, Eva Kramer
July 12, 1941
From: Pearl Harbor, Honolulu, HI
To: Chippewa Falls, WI

In response to the closure of all German consulates in the United States, the Axis powers reciprocated with a near-identical policy. Roosevelt, still appalled at the sinking of the *Robin Moor*, issued a special message to Congress in which he labeled Germany "an international outlaw." He warned that the United

States would not "yield use of the high seas to Germany" and demanded Germany pay "full reparations for the losses and damages suffered."[255]

The following day, on June 22, residents in Chippewa Falls were stunned to read the overly enlarged newspaper headline, "**GERMANY INVADES RUSSIA.**" In an attack code-named Operation Barbarossa, more than three million German and Axis soldiers invaded the Soviet Union over an 1,800-mile front. Hitler's plan called for a three-pronged attack: capture Ukraine in the south, Moscow to the east and Leningrad in the north. The speed and brutality of Hitler's initial blitzkrieg had taken the Soviet Union off guard. By July 1, it had been reported that "Leningrad was in flames," "Germany was halfway to Moscow" and the Soviet Union was "Asking the US for Help."[256]

With the *Robin Moor* incident seeming like a distant memory, Roosevelt scrambled to determine an official position on the Soviet Union, as administration officials quickly inquired into the feasibility of placing military orders through the lend-lease program. In the interim, Roosevelt did make it known that he had no interest in remaining neutral and promised "whatever aid that could be given," including permission to allow "US vessels to carry arms to Russians" via the port of Vladivostok in the Pacific. As for additional lend-lease orders, domestic production wasn't keeping pace as it was.[257] Out of survival, Soviet leader Joseph Stalin ordered his people to adopt a "scorched earth" and "universal guerilla warfare" policy. "In case of a forced retreat," Stalin proclaimed, "the enemy must not be left a single engine, railway car, pound of grain, or gallon of fuel."[258]

During his Fourth of July radio address, Roosevelt asked the American people for a "united defense." "We need not the loyalty and unity alone," the president implored, "we need speed and efficiency and toil" in defense manufacturing and munitions factories. "I tell the American people solemnly," he concluded, "that the United States will never survive as a happy and fertile oasis of liberty in the midst of a desert of dictatorship."[259]

Days later, Roosevelt sent naval forces to "Occupy Iceland." The goal was to relieve and supplant the British there, as a strategic way to protect the "seas between the United States and all other strategic outposts." In another special message to Congress, Roosevelt announced that the nation could not permit Germany to use Iceland as "air or naval bases for eventual attack against the Western Hemisphere."[260]

Published reports stated that, rather than stopping with just Iceland, the United States had also been sending money and workers to Scotland and Northern Ireland, in order to construct bases there. The response by the

Axis powers was mixed. Germany remained silent, whereas Japan labeled it "warlike." Still enraged about Roosevelt's decision to still allow U.S. merchant vessels to carry guns to the Soviet Union via the Pacific Ocean, Japan announced it was "studying" the feasibility of extending its territorial waters so it could block U.S. shipments to the Soviet port of Vladivostok.[261]

In the month since his last letter, Harry had successfully tested into the rank of fireman first class (F1C). On June 20, the studious sailor had managed to score the highest out of all exam-takers aboard ship. Harry had quickly become an expert in engine room knowledge and was thriving in his new quarterly assignment in the ship's machine shop. While all firemen's uniforms contained a red branch mark on the left shoulder, a fireman first class was distinguished by three stripes on the left cuff of the sleeve.

Career wise, Harry had been awarded the highest enlisted man's rank for a sailor who worked belowdecks. Any future promotion would elevate Harry from enlisted status to noncommissioned officer, or petty officer, status. As a petty officer, a sailor would be taken off the quarterly assignment rotation and assigned to a specific department belowdecks in a role such as boilermaker, machinist's mate, water tender, metalsmith, molder or motor machinist's mate. As Harry continued his job training throughout the various departments, the machine shop was quickly becoming his favorite.[262]

Supplementing these professional advancements, Harry had begun to socialize more with his fellow sailors during liberty. One outing included a beach party with a group of fifty sailors. The men boarded a narrow-gauge train, operated by the Oahu Railway and Land Company (OR&L), and traveled twenty to thirty miles to the Island of Oahu's leeward western shore. Their destination was a census-designated place named Nanakuli, which is Hawaiian for "to look at the knee." The area was well known for its five-hundred-foot concave beach, situated between two limestone points. Aside from having far fewer people to compete with, as compared to Waikiki Beach, Nanakuli is known for its hot and dry climate, high surfs, strong currents and lack of shade from the sun.[263] The adventurous Harry was thrilled to get the full Nanakuli experience, including an overly dark tan, hours of swimming and wave diving and the consumption of eleven bottles of Coca-Cola, to quench his seemingly endless thirst from the heat.[264]

Harry also frequently attended the Church of Christ, Scientist, in downtown Honolulu. Located at 1508 Punahou Street, the historic church was situated some ten miles east of Pearl Harbor Naval Station and just three miles north of Waikiki Beach. Designed by legendary architect Hart

Designed by architect Hart Wood, the First Church of Christ, Scientist, is a famous landmark in Honolulu, seen here circa 1940. *Author's collection.*

Wood in 1923, the picturesque exterior of the church features "coarse lava-rock walls and a steep, shingled, able roof with overhanging eaves" and is finished with a "Tudor Gothic entrance and spire."[265] Wood was well known in Hawaii for being the "first architect to meld Asian and Western forms" and became "one of the giants of Hawaii's regionalist design movements." In addition to the Church of Christ, Scientist, Wood's distinctive "Hawaiian style" was applied to both the "Alexander and Baldwin Building and the Board of Water Supply Administration building" in Honolulu.[266]

Hart Wood and his family were also members of the church. The Wood family was composed of Hart; his wife, Jessie; and their four adult sons, Hart Jr., Thomas, Benton and Kenneth. With their three grown children having moved away and their fourth busy in college, the gracious Hart and Jessie hosted Harry and a few other Church of Christ, Scientist sailors at their house for food and fellowship. Their home, built near the base of a sloping hill named Round Top at 2512 Manoa Road on Honolulu's east side, was also designed by the famous architect. The upstairs attic served as Hart's personal design office.

The Woods, meanwhile, were so impressed by the twenty-one-year-old fireman first class that they gave him an extensive driving tour of the island.[267] The naturally friendly Harry, with his midwestern charm and sensibilities, had memorably endeared himself to one of Hawaii's most famous and culturally acclaimed residents.

Dear Mother,

I was very glad to get your mail....Sorry you had to wait so long for mine. I ought to be more careful of that.

My studying is over...since I made Fireman First Class. Yes, I passed... got the highest mark with a 3.84 out of 4.0 possible. I'll be getting sixty dollars a month now! I haven't added on to my allotment yet, as I'm building up the total amount to a hundred dollars...in case I get leave I'll have money on hand.

Am sure getting along swell in the machine shop....I like it better than any other station. I have a lathe of my own which I've been running steadily...but also run jobs on the big drill press and machines.

I went to a beach party at Nānākuli and had a wonderful time. You should now see how dark my skin is after playing on the beach under the Hawaiian sunshine. I lost my old swimming suit so I bought some new Hawaiian trunks. Boy they're swell and it didn't take me long to break them in! They are a green color with a pattern of seaweed, with little fish swimming through it, outlined in white. No kidding, they look natty—(not nutty).

The party consisted of 50 men and we left at 0800 by train. It is 20 miles to Nānākuli. The beach out there is simply marvelous. The sand is shining white and fine. The surf was perfect. The waves would start breaking about two hundred feet from shore and come rolling in about six feet high. Several of us played in them for hours and believe me it exhausts a person. We run into the water and a fast booming surf will hit you above the knees and knock you flat. I also consumed seven hot dogs, three apples, and eleven bottles of Coca-Cola during the day. Most of the others, however, thought they were enjoying themselves by getting drunk...didn't know what was really going on. The two other boys with me went for the pleasure of swimming and had a swell day.

I had a chance to go to church and after the service, a Mr. and Mrs. Wood invited three other sailors and I to their home for lunch. Golly were they swell people....We get to do that nearly every Sunday. The home is a beautiful place built up a slope. The yard contains half a dozen different fruit-bearing trees. Mrs. Wood showed us bunches of bananas near the back porch. For dinner, we had salad, cold meats, jams, rolls, and delicious chocolate cake.

They drove us nearly all the way around the island. Golly it was sure swell of them. He is an architect and built the church. They have lived here for over twenty years but travel to Boston every so often as he has something to do with the publication committee.

They have four boys but all of them are away except the youngest who is in college. All of the boys are expert surf board riders and have won several medals in swimming meets.

Well, it's time to go....Aloha to all. Thanks a lot Grandma and Dad for the letters.

Harry

————

Letter No. 29: Harry Kramer to his mother, Eva Kramer
August 5, 1941
From: Pearl Harbor, Honolulu, HI
To: Chippewa Falls, WI

Throughout the rest of summer, Hitler's army pushed deep into Soviet territory. German land forces neared Leningrad to the north and Kiev, Ukraine, in the south, while the Luftwaffe bombed Moscow to the east. On July 19, the *Chippewa Herald-Telegram*'s front-page banner read, "GATE TO MOSCOW OPEN," as Stalin had ordered nearly four million men to be held back to defend the fledgling capital.[268]

In East Asia, rumors swirled that Japan was contemplating an invasion of the Soviet Union from its eastern flank.[269] In reality, Japan's intention was to take control of remaining areas in French Indochina from the hands of the Vichy government. In particular, Saigon, Vietnam, and Bangkok, Thailand, were viewed as strategic staging areas for eventual attacks against Singapore (British), the Dutch East Indies (Netherlands) and the Philippines (United States). On July 25, the United States learned that Japan had mobilized an additional one million men into its army's ranks.[270]

In response, Roosevelt issued an executive order freezing all Japanese credits and assets in the United States. Great Britain and the Dutch East Indies followed his lead, resulting in Japan losing an estimated three-fourths of its total economic trade overseas.[271] The next day, Roosevelt announced the mobilization and federalization of the armies of the Philippines, an unorganized territory of the United States. Roosevelt named General Douglas MacArthur, a decorated war hero from World War I, commander of the United States Army Forces in the Far East (USAFFE).[272] By early

August, the U.S. Navy had sent warships near Australia to partake in a "training cruise," much to the dismay and protest of Japan.[273]

On the American home front, communities across the country began participating in various fundraisers and scrap metal drives associated with the war production effort. One of the most familiar and successful organizations to fundraise was the United Service Organization for National Defense, or USO. Its mission was to provide necessary "social, religious, recreational, and educational services" to those in the service. The group had recently been founded by social reformer Mary Shotwell Ingraham, in direct response to President Roosevelt's call for such a group.

In partnership with the federal government, the USO had built or leased "360 service clubs in 125 defense areas throughout the nation and on overseas bases." By mid-July, the USO had announced that it would be working with every municipality, church and civic organization that was interested in Chippewa County. Chippewa Falls resident Gerald O. Thorpe, who lived at 722 West Willow Street, served as the USO's county treasurer and was responsible for forwarding all monies raised locally on to the national organization.[274]

Residents of Chippewa County were also asked to donate in a highly publicized aluminum scrap metal drive, to raise much-needed materials for the national defense manufacturing program. The event was organized by the recently created Chippewa County Defense Council, which consisted of representatives of "civic, fraternal, veteran, and other organizations" and was chaired by Chippewa Falls mayor John Zesiger. When the drive ended after nine days, Mayor Zesiger happily proclaimed that a whopping 6,635 pounds of aluminum, or 3.3 tons, had been donated. Leading the pack were the residents of Chippewa Falls, who had donated just over one-third of the total aluminum haul.[275]

While it's not known if Harry was aware of the USO's efforts, he certainly was benefiting from their results. In his most recent letter home, Harry eagerly shared his delight in the recent opening of a new recreational center at Pearl Harbor Naval Station. Named the Bloch Recreation Center and Arena, after a commandant of the base, the facility was centrally built near the main gate. It could accommodate "6,000 spectators for stage, boxing ring and movie shows," which were often put on by the USO. The facility also provided a "large basketball court, ten bowling alleys, six pool tables, reading and writing rooms, a canteen and beer bar, and a dance floor and lanai."[276] Harry playfully gave his mother a detailed tour of the new facility, including a rundown of the large volume of food that the hungry sailor had eaten from the building's canteen.[277]

Harry also wrote that he had recently returned to Nanakuli, on the western shore. On this trip, Harry stated that the visit had been part of an official U.S. Navy retreat with five hundred other sailors. The military operated an outpost there called Camp Andrews, a rustic facility located across from the Nānākuli train depot. Although the men were technically on duty, the greater purpose of the camp was for the men to relax. Harry and the rest would wear their white uniforms to and from the camp but wore navy-issued swimming shorts on arrival. While there, most of the daily protocols were suspended, including general quarters drills and morning reveille.[278] The men simply "slept, ate, swam, lounged, played games, and hiked." In Harry's case, a large and distinctive 860-foot hill, called Pu'u'ohulu Kai, beckoned him and a few other sailors to hike its base.

The six-mile trek left quite an impression, as it reminded him of spending time with his hometown friends, including Mort, Jack and Loyal. Harry was thrilled to learn that Loyal had recently moved to Southern California, where he had been hired to work in Consolidated Aircraft's airplane factory. Harry looked forward to meeting up with Loyal next time he and the *California* visited Long Beach. As for Mort, Harry still hadn't received any letters from him since he joined the U.S. Army Air Corps.[279]

Although he missed home, Harry continued to treasure his time in Hawaii. He spent his days swimming, reading, scrapbooking, attending church and socializing with the Wood family. Professionally, the hardworking fireman first class was respected and well liked by his crewmates. They fondly nicknamed him Duke Wellington, based on his middle name. Presumably, the nickname was inspired by a combination of the Duke of Wellington, an eighteenth-century British commander who defeated Napoleon Bonaparte at Waterloo,[280] and Duke Ellington, an African American jazz orchestra leader whose biggest hit, "Take the A Train," finished eighth on *Billboard Magazine*'s top one hundred songs in 1941.[281] Either way, Harry loved it.

Additionally, in a rare display of candor to his mother, Harry made it known that he had a celebrity crush on a Hollywood actress named Olivia de Havilland. The twenty-five-year-old starlet had earned critical acclaim for her performance as Melanie Hamilton in *Gone with the Wind* (1939), for which she received an Academy Award nomination in the category of Best Actress in a Supporting Role.[282] De Haviland was slimly built, stood 5′4″ and possessed both dark brown hair and eyes. In her most recent release, she starred alongside James Cagney in the hit romantic comedy *The Strawberry Blonde* (1941).

Dear Mother,

I'm writing this letter in the most beautiful recreation center I've ever been. This new building has been open only a few days. Boy Oh Boy! I was amazed when I got here....Still acting like a kid over a new toy. Everything was built for the convenience of we boys. Upstairs there is one huge room containing many new billiard tables at which one may play cards, checkers, write, or read magazines. All the furniture is the latest style and is upholstered in bright blue leather. Comfortable—HA—you merely sit down and your eyes automatically close and go wandering in slumberland. Well, almost!

Next we go down to the main deck where...the bowling alleys are, which are always crowded. Now if you wish to get candy, ice cream, pop, pineapple juice, chewing gum, peanuts, or sandwiches...step into the large canteen and order up. Now listen Kramer you've already had three cheese sandwiches, four bottles of pineapple juice, and a half pint of ice cream, so it's not wise to get anymore!

Yes mother, I was talking to myself. If you would taste that Dole Pineapple Juice....Hard to give up with just one bottle. On the opposite side of the game rooms, there is a separate section with a seating capacity of four to six thousand men for boxing matches, movies, or programs. This place is the very tops!

Yes, I've been on a weekend camping trip too, at Nānākuli Beach about twenty miles from Pearl Harbor. Golly that was paradise. There were five hundred of us. As soon as we arrived by train, we got a tent, two cots, and freedom from regulation of any kind. We could wear anything we pleased, except just our skivvies shorts. Most of the men wore their swimming trunks from the time they got out of their cots until bed. We could lay around camp drinking pop or eating and if we decided to take a swim just get up enough ambition to walk across the highway and dive into the big surf in the ocean. Boy what a time! Three of us took a six mile hike around the base of a mountain off the main highway. It made me think of being with Mort Anderson again. You sure surprised me when telling of his arrival at home...Sure like to see him again. This Sunday I dressed up in a brand new suit....Planning to go to church to meet Mr. and Mrs. Hart Wood again. Something came up which detained me and I was too late to go out there. It was something rather unusual and I'd like to tell you about...but am unable due to military reasons. I had an experience which I'll never forget and hope to do again someday.

"Reader's Digest" is down to half price for enlisted men....Going to subscribe to it. Lately, I've had a chance to work on my scrapbook....Get

a lot of happy times out of it. I'm making it in sections. One is made up of pictures of the fleet, one of the airplanes and data, one of the navy picture jokes, and one for my favorite movie star, *Olivia De Havilland!*

Snapshot of Harry's celebrity crush, Hollywood actress Olivia de Havilland, circa 1940. *Author's collection.*

Would you like to look at it if I send it back? Loyal Lubach is not far from my home base is he? If I were back there I'd look him up. If he gets a job in a plane factory that will be nice. That's what I'd like to do if I was not in the navy. Liking planes...I'd be right at home in a Douglas plant.

By the way I've got some nice snapshots. Pictures of me taking my place in society on crowded Waikiki Beach!

After drinking another bottle of pineapple juice...going back to the Prune Barge—14 decks and a straw bottom. Give my love to Grandma and Dad.

Aloha,

Harry

P.S. On board I'm known only as Duke Wellington! Will not be changed until further notice.

Letter No. 30: Harry Kramer to his mother, Eva Kramer
October 5, 1941
From: Long Beach, CA
To: Chippewa Falls, WI

In the two months since Harry's last letter, Germany had successfully cut off Leningrad, thus initiating a long-term blockade and "siege" of the Soviet Union's second-largest city.[283] Japan, meanwhile, was rumored to be preparing an invasion of Thailand, which incensed the British due to their strategic interests in nearby Singapore, an island nation off the southern tip of Malaysia.[284]

On August 9 and 10, 1941, Roosevelt and Churchill secretly met aboard the USS *Augusta* near Newfoundland, Canada. Churchill hoped to convince Roosevelt to officially enter the war. Roosevelt, for his part, wanted assurances that Britain was not party to any secret treaties that would enable it to add additional territories after the war. Roosevelt also wanted clarification and specifics related to Britain's repayment for the use of lend-lease materials. Above all else, the president hoped that the eventual press coverage of the meeting would help sway American public opinion toward more intervention.[285]

Although neither man fully achieved his goal, the conference did produce a written draft of eight common principles that both nations would commit to after the war. In this Atlantic Charter, both leaders agreed not to add new territories; to make no territorial changes without the permission of the peoples concerned; to respect the rights of peoples to reintroduce their own forms of self-government; to allow each to seek out raw materials; to promote worldwide collaboration to improve labor, economic and social security; to look for peace once "Nazi tyranny" had been destroyed; to promote the freedom of the seas; and lastly, to disarm aggressors in order to guarantee future peace in the world.[286]

Details from the charter appeared prominently under a banner headline on August 14. The new "Joint War, Peace Program against Nazi Tyranny" quickly elicited a response from Germany.[287] "If the so-called democracies want Germany disarmed, let them come and get our arms," a Nazi source was quoted as saying.[288]

Despite no mention of Japan, the East Asian country took immediate offense to the document. A Japanese diplomat in London said that the omission of any reference to his country implied that Japan was, in fact, "one of the main points of discussion" at the conference.[289]

Japan maintained that it was not fearful of Great Britain's influence in the South Pacific or its "posturing." Responding to calls for the Japanese to change their policies in the Far East, Lieutenant Colonel Kunio Akiyama stated, "Churchill cannot change the attitude or policies of Japan." What did worry Japan, however, was Britain's ever-growing alliance with the United States. "What we observe with greater concern," Akiyama added, "is this ulterior motive…to induce the United States into war."[290]

Roosevelt continued to insist that the United States was no nearer to war now than it was prior. In an attempt to better coordinate the distribution of materials and commodities related to the country's national defense, Roosevelt tapped Vice President Henry Wallace to chair the Supply Priorities and Allocation Board (SPAB).[291] The president also called on the navy to improve and expand naval ports in Iceland and signed an executive order to halt the "8-hour work day law" for mechanics and laborers working on select projects ordered by the war department.[292] In short, Roosevelt wanted faster production and quicker shipments.

Assisting Roosevelt were significant votes cast by lawmakers in Congress. To fund the massive military expansion, Congress passed a record-setting tax increase on individuals, married couples, heads of households and inheritors of wealth. The progressive tax code consisted of thirty-two brackets, escalated from a 10 percent minimum tax to a maximum tax rate of 81 percent. The plan also included new surtaxes on corporate profits and estate and gift inheritances. Roosevelt promptly signed the measure.[293]

By early September, tensions on the high seas between Germany and the United States had reached a near-boiling point. The USS *Greer*, a naval destroyer, was targeted by a Nazi U-boat while carrying mail and passengers to Iceland. In response to the near miss, the *Greer* dropped depth charges in an attempt to hit the submarine. Roosevelt acknowledged that this wasn't the first time the *Greer* had been fired on.[294]

In the coming days, Germany would sink two United States–affiliated merchant ships: SS *Steel Seafarer*, near Iceland, and SS *Sessa*, in the Red Sea. Since 1939, Germany had been suspected of sinking five U.S. merchant vessels, resulting in the deaths of at least sixty-five Americans.[295] A furious Roosevelt had seen enough.

On September 11, President Roosevelt gave the United States Navy a "shoot first" order to protect all American shipping interests in western waters.

Opposition to Roosevelt's shoot first order came swiftly from various lawmakers, including U.S. Senator Robert M. La Follete Jr. of Wisconsin. He charged the president with breaking the anti-war pledge he had campaigned on. La Follette compared the president's actions to that of Woodrow Wilson leading up to America's entry in World War I and accused Roosevelt of "short-circuiting Congress's constitutional power to declare war" when he ordered the navy to initiate conflict.[296]

Joining La Follette in staunch opposition was Charles Lindbergh, who predicted that the president's actions were moving the country toward dictatorship. He maintained that the administration might soon end both free speech and democratically held elections. Lindbergh's dark rhetoric came on the heels of a recent speech he gave in Des Moines, Iowa, where he alleged that "the British, the Jewish, and the Roosevelt Administration" were among the most notable groups pressuring the United States toward war with Germany. The once universally adored aviator had morphed into one of the most polarizing figures in American political society.[297]

In Chippewa Falls, community efforts to support the nation's buildup of military defenses continued. In addition to the post office, businesses agreed to sell defense bonds and stamps. Defense bonds, similar to modern-day government savings bonds, could be purchased with face amounts ranging from $18.75 to $10,000 (with investment maturity at ten years). Another option was for citizens to acquire individual defense stamps, which resembled postage stamps. These could be purchased in smaller denominations and were saved by affixing them in a special war defense stamp booklet. Once the booklet was filled, it could be exchanged for a larger-denomination defense bond. Mayor John Zesiger, a big proponent of the two options, issued a proclamation establishing "Retail for Defense Week." In partnership with the Chippewa Falls Chamber of Commerce, the mayor urged "all of our citizens to cooperate and to participate in this fine effort to aid and support the National Defense Program."[298]

In addition to the bond and stamp drive, a local group of pilots sought to organize themselves as part of a "Wisconsin Air Squadron" for home military defense purposes. Spurred by Governor Julius Heil's call for such a civilian air squadron, members of the Indian Head Flying Club, composed of twenty-five pilots from the Chippewa Falls and Eau Claire area, petitioned to be a part of the program. The group was based out of an airport near Lake Hallie, and tentative plans called for it to be used for domestic aerial reconnaissance. At no direct financial cost to the state taxpayer, each aviator would volunteer their own time, fuel and airplane. John Ritzinger, Chippewa County clerk of court and representative of the club, had traveled to Madison to confer with state officials on the details of the venture.[299]

By October, Harry and the *California* had sailed back to California. It had been exactly one month since Harry's last letter home, as the maturing sailor continued to forge his own independence. Harry candidly admitted that his letter writing had begun to wane, as his newfound interest in playing tennis had been occupying his liberty time. While aboard ship, the musically inclined Harry was always a frequent participant in the impromptu "sing song" events above decks.[300]

The excitement of returning to California, however, had rejuvenated his letter-writing spirit, as Harry was eager to share good news with his mother. While docked in Northern California, Harry hoped to once again meet up with Mildred Grant, the older widow and Church of Christ, Scientist member. She had recently relocated from Washington State to the San Francisco Bay area. More than anyone, Harry couldn't wait to see his relatives living in Long Beach and La Jolla. In particular, Harry desired to spend as much time as he could with his second cousins Gene Durfee and Glen Liddiard. Both men were similar in age and shared many of the same interests, including music and airplanes.[301]

But unexpected events back home also drew Harry's attention. His older brother, Robert, a mechanic at the Chippewa Valley Auto Company in Chippewa Falls, suffered a serious injury to "one of his eyes when it was struck by a small piece of steel." He was admitted into St. Joseph's Hospital, where doctors were able to save the eye.[302]

Dear Mother,

Your letter came and it was enjoyed.…Been so long since I've written. In this heat one has a tendency to feel tired all the time. When I go on liberty I feel pretty frisky but then I am so busy playing games I don't take time for writing either. Tonight, however, I feel gay as a 21 year old kid in love so will start the ink flowing. First, I'll tell you the grand news. I'm going back to the states—and am getting four days leave to see the Liddiards. Golly am I happy. I will arrive in San Francisco…be there three days…then going to Long Beach. Mrs. Mildred Grant, whom I visit so much in Seattle, has moved there so I'll get a chance to see her.

It's been nine months since my visit to La Jolla.…Anxious to get back. I've been thinking of the boys [Glen Liddiard and Gene Durfee] *and wondering what they've been doing. They showed me a wonderful time.… Been thinking about it ever since. Great Aunt Minnie will be happy too. Boy oh boy just picture me striding up to the Fleet Locker Club opening my locker and laying out my civilian clothes again. Putting on my green sport pants and best polo shirt, I'll sally forth on the road of adventure and romance. Well, not so sure about the last!!*

It was quite a surprise to learn of Robert's accident. I was so thankful that he did not lose his eye…and all will be well. How I'd love to walk in on Robert at his place unannounced. He'd be surprised wouldn't he? Well, I'd enjoy it.…Hope someday to get some leave. The little fellows will be little no more. You make me laugh out loud when I read of those witty things they say…like David wanting his Dad to go back to the hospital! You told me Gerald had written to me on an envelope and it was enclosed with your letter. I am sorry to say that I did not find it.…Maybe forgot to put it in? Send it next time.…I'll write him a note in return.

Went on a shopping tour.…Bought a heavy duty cot. The nights are warm and it's too hot below decks. But sleeping topside is heavenly with a cool breeze blowing across your face and the stars shining overhead. Sometimes

*one of those five minute wind squalls will come up and a hundred guys...
can be seen scurrying for cover under turrets, boats, etc., dragging mattresses
along. I used to sleep on the hard deck...but now with my cot—oh boy what
a luxury. We also bought a softball to use topside after working hours. A lot
of boys play catch....Have to be careful about losing the ball overboard.
Another one of my hobbies is tennis. I got a racket a week ago....With
all the nice courts around here we have fun. Have also been using a new
swimming pool in the yards. Usually I play tennis for a couple of hours, then
swim. Oh yes, and eat sandwiches and pineapple juice!!*

 *One night while at sea we had a big sing song party on the boat deck.
It all started casual....Two or three musicians brought their instruments
topside to practice and get fresh air. Soon the small crowd (including me)
grew to a big one and more and more musicians joined. A big full moon
hung overhead...with me singing my head off with a rolling deck under my
feet helping me keep time. When it comes to popular music and sing song
contests I'm always present. The band played till dark and practically wore
themselves out. Should have heard us sing "California, Here We Come."*

 *Was glad to get Mort's address as I'd never heard from him since he left
for Mississippi. I'd be mighty happy if Dad got that nice job...but must
not feel too badly if he doesn't. Tell him I missed those big red tomatoes
from his garden ever so much.*

 Love to all,

 Harry

———

Letter No. 31: Harry Kramer to his mother, Eva Kramer
October 30, 1941
From: Long Beach, CA
To: Chippewa Falls, WI

As summer gave way to fall, Germany expanded its offensive into the Soviet
Union. With his army reportedly just thirty-eight miles outside of Moscow,
Hitler wanted to "smash Russia before winter." Stalin was adamant that his
country would prevail as the "entire Soviet nation is being mobilized to meet
the assault."[303]

 In Washington, D.C., Roosevelt asked Congress to revise the Neutrality
Act to allow merchant ships to arm themselves against U-boat attacks. The
president was adamant that U-boats would only increase their attacks and

wanted to provide the merchant ships with the means of self-defense. Then, on October 17, Germany torpedoed an American destroyer off Iceland. The USS *Kearny* survived the attack, but eleven sailors were killed and another twenty-two were injured.[304] The House of Representatives quickly voted to revise the Neutrality Act and allow the Roosevelt administration to arm merchant vessels. The proposal passed 259 to 138.[305] Six days later, the War Department announced that it would be tripling the size of the Army's Air Corps program and rushed to have four hundred thousand men in its ranks by next June.[306]

On October 27, Roosevelt gave his Navy Day address, in which he chastised Germany for causing the deaths of the sailors aboard the *Kearny*. "Shooting has started…and America has been attacked," an impassioned Roosevelt conveyed. Citing a phrase from U.S. naval tradition, he added, "Damn the torpedos; full speed ahead!"[307] In response to the speech, U.S. Senator Alexander Wiley of Wisconsin stated, "I got the impression that the President was ready to go to war." The next day, Wiley announced that he would oppose any proposed changes to the Neutrality Act, as it was one of the last acts standing in the way of "America's full involvement in the war."[308] The bill's passage remained murky, despite a White House poll showing fifty-five senators (out of ninety-six total) were likely to vote yes.[309]

Japan's political situation had also changed. Prime Minister Fumimaro Konoe, as well as his third cabinet, submitted his resignation to leader Emperor Hirohito. While Konoe had been instrumental in Japan's invasion of China, his inability to resolve tensions with the United States led to his ouster. Emperor Hirohito replaced Konoe with General Hideki Tojo. Despite Tojo's verbal desire for improved U.S. relations, the new fifty-six-year-old prime minister saw Japan as being at a "crossroads in her history." Tojo believed Japan was in danger of "encirclement by foreign powers." He feared that the United States would eventually be granted coastal access in eastern Russia, as payment for the lend-lease military supplies they were sending the Soviets. Tojo called on both the Japanese military and the civilian population to come together and form an "Iron Unity" against any forms of encirclement.[310]

But it was the attack on the *Kearny* that established Germany as the United States' primary geopolitical concern. Having returned from a six-week stint of sea duty in the Pacific Fleet as a marine corps reserve air officer, Republican congressman Melvin Maas of Minnesota was confident of America's naval might. Maas observed that Japan was "deathly afraid" of the U.S. Pacific Fleet and believed that the Western Hemisphere "is in no danger from Japanese aggression." Maas surmised, "No navy could get to Panama without passing Hawaii, and no navy could get past Hawaii."[311]

Harry was excited to be back in San Francisco but also disappointed in his inability to connect with Mrs. Mildred Grant. Nonetheless, Harry took the opportunity to place a phone call to George and Louise Simpson and their daughter Jean. Harry never forgot how wonderful a time the Simpsons had shown him at their home in Montana and quickly found himself reliving memories of the good meals he had staying at their home.[312]

But Harry seemed happiest when his ship anchored in Long Beach. Harry traveled the one hundred miles south, by bus, to visit his great-aunt Minnie's side of the family in La Jolla, or suburban San Diego. Once again, he was reunited with Glen Liddiard and Morien Eugene Durfee Jr. or Gene, as he was known. The three young men explored San Diego and went bowling at the famous "Tower Bowl," a recently opened entertainment complex featuring twenty-eight bowling lanes.[313]

When back in Long Beach, Harry split his liberty with Gene Durfee Jr. or

the family of Theodore and Alice Marie Hribal. The son of another well-known and successful architect, Gene Durfee Jr. was able to maintain his own residence in Long Beach, where Harry marveled at the twenty-year-old's extensive record collection. Harry also expressed serious concern for the health of Gene's father. Architect Morien Eugene Durfee Sr. had been managing a serious illness for several months and was preparing to undergo a medical procedure to remove a suspicious, and likely cancerous, growth related to one of his eyes.[314]

Living nearby was the Hribal family, whose matriarch, Alice Marie, was the granddaughter of Great Aunt Minnie. Theodore and Alice Marie had four children together, including Hope and Alice Theresa, who were closest to Harry's age. Harry glowed over the intelligence of the fourteen-year-old Alice Theresa, who would come home

Harry took a final photo in La Jolla, California, prior to his reboarding of the USS *California*, circa 1941. *Author's collection.*

from school and quiz him in the subjects of algebra and Spanish. Just as Harry had developed his own life in Hawaii, the young sailor had become a welcome addition to his mother's extended family.[315]

As Harry embarked for a return voyage to Pearl Harbor, he learned that he had been once again assigned to the "Fresh Water Hold," located deep within the bowels of the ship.[316]

Dear Mother,

You are waiting to hear about my visit…I suppose. I have certainly been on the go…every minute of liberty. I wrote in my last letter about stopping in San Francisco and visiting Mrs. Mildred Grant, but was disappointed in not being able to get in touch with her. It was impossible to let her know beforehand…as the liberty list were made up just a few hours ahead of schedule. After calling her place for the 5th time…the idea popped into my head to phone the Simpsons long distance. Golly those few moments waiting for the call to go through had me on edge with excitement. The element of surprise was enjoyed by all…with everyone at home eating supper. Ah! I would have liked to have had my legs stuck under a table holding a steaming home-cooked meal! Well, I did fare well at the YMCA in Frisco. It's the best "Y" I've been in and…[the] restaurant is swell. Things are quite cheap yet tasty. And their rooms! Boy I really enjoyed that big soft mattress and slept like a baby till they held reveille on me the next morning at 06:30.

It took us one day to come from Frisco.…I had duty so could not go over. Several times I stuck my head out a port and gazed longingly at the distant buildings in Long Beach. All of us had four day leave chits [passes] *signed. I got a shock to learn that all leave had been canceled and all men who were on their way home had telegrams saying to return immediately. That same day I took a 5 PM bus from Long Beach to La Jolla…arrived by 8 o'clock. It was wonderful to see everyone again. Told them I came down for just the four hours…had to take the 0130 bus from San Diego that same night. The boys drove me down and we looked around town before I left. Got back to Long Beach again the next morning at 0415 and my liberty ended on the dock at 0700. As soon as I got back to the ship I found out we could put-in for a 48 hour liberty and that's what I did. I was again on that bus for La Jolla but this time to stay longer.*

Well, all I can say is that I can hardly describe the wonderful time I had. The boys, Glen Liddiard and Gene Durfee, took me to San Diego and went to a brand new super bowling center called the "Tower." There are twenty eight alleys side by side. In the back there are huge soda fountains, entertaining rooms, etc. Talk about modernistic design! We could hardly get in, it was packed. Got to bed at 0130 and didn't even move an eyelash till Glen woke me at 1100 the next day. Boy those big red sliced tomatoes cousin Ruth Liddiard fixed up every meal—mmm—Had so much to talk about to Great Aunt Minnie and everyone that it took me an hour to eat. Or else I just ate a lot…don't know which. We boys bowled at a place one block from the house and I sure had fun. I'm going to buy a pair of bowling shoes next time I go.

Sunday afternoon, Cousin Ruth drove me to Long Beach in their new 1941 Dodge. Great Aunt Minnie came along. The Durfees and Hribals were all together with me. They drove me down to my locker club and I said goodbye about 9 o'clock that evening. Hurrying into my uniform again I got to the dock just before 10 o'clock at which time I thought my leave was up. I got to talking with a shore patrol and he said that all 48's were up at 8 o'clock instead of 10. Boy…I nearly fell through the dock…realizing I was two hours over. I was kind of scared but…tried to know that it would not be so bad. When the ten o'clock launch came in and I went back to the ship, stepped up on the quarterdeck and stuck my card in the box. No one checked me for being late…so I went to see the liberty petty officer in my division. He said that the schedule had been changed…and that liberty was not up till seven in the morning. Golly I let out a big sigh knowing I was not over…but in fact the first one back aboard from my division.

The next morning we were told that liberty would be daily from 1 PM to 8 AM the next morning. I've been going ashore every other day while still anchored here. For a while it was expected that we'd get underway any minute. Have been seeing a lot of the Hribals lately. Go over every time I'm ashore in the afternoon then walk back seven blocks to Durfee's and see Gene. Hope and Alice Hribal are going to school, but get home early in the afternoon. I've been getting a lot of practice trying to work out some of the Algebra problems Alice gives me. I've forgotten a lot of math, as I've never used it enough. Then after an hour's work on that she starts in on me with her Spanish book!! Have a lot of fun though.

Gene and I went to a radio store…and browsed around the huge phonograph record collection. I bought two records—"Intermezzo" and "Piano Concerto in B Flat"—They are very popular songs taken from original symphony pieces. Gene played the original "Piano Concerto" by Tchaikovsky and it is really beautiful. There are four records to the original set that costs $4.50. Gene says someday he'll get it. The "Piano Concerto"

I got is just a single record and is a popular condensation of the others. By the way, Gene has 1500 records at home. Some selection I'd say. I'm going over tomorrow and will hear some more. One of the boys got payed off so they put me back down in the Fresh Water Hold and because the radio doesn't work so far below the water line I'm starved for music.

Morien Eugene Durfee Sr., Gene's dad, has to have another operation on his eye. It's certainly too bad. They say there's a little growth starting and has to come out. It may not be so bad this time but they can't tell. He has been feeling kind of weak and tired so they want to take out that part so he can get well again. I hope everything will turn out all right. He has surely been through a lot and his work has been none too good.

How is Robert? Feeling better I hope. Is he working full-time yet? Will be so glad to hear that everything is working out all right. I was so happy to get Gerald's envelope and see his drawings.

I had the locker club send my winter suit home as I never used it here in this climate and have my other lighter sport clothes. Also sent a package home containing all of those swell letters you sent the past few months and the little gold wrist watch. I cannot wear it as it is too delicate and the fastenings are always coming loose after the jewelers fix them.

You asked about my allotment. I made out a new one starting about a month ago for $20.00…to run for two years. I would have made it more but I wanted to build up an account here on the books so after that I can send extra home by money order. How much do I have in the bank now?

Well, I believe I'm running low on words so will close for tonight. Give my love to Grandma, Dad, and Robert and family.

Love,
Harry

———

Letter No. 32: Harry Kramer to his mother, Eva Kramer
November 17, 1941
From: Pearl Harbor, Honolulu, HI
To: Chippewa Falls, WI

On Halloween, a German U-boat dealt another stunning blow to the United States government. An American Clemson-class U.S. Navy destroyer, USS *Reuben James*, was sunk near Iceland. The surprise left one hundred Americans dead, including ninety-two sailors, seven officers and one passenger. The vessel had been the third U.S. ship fired on within a span of two months. Roosevelt's public response was that it would have "no change" on America's immediate relations with Germany. However, the president urged Congress to quickly pass changes to the Neutrality Act.[317]

Although the human loss on *Reuben James* had been significant, the sinking did not lead to mass public cries for retaliation. One New York House member announced a bill that would sever all relations between the two countries, but it didn't gain traction. One British newspaper bluntly observed, "America has not yet declared war; but Hitler has."[318]

The politics surrounding America's increased global footprint remained dicey, as Roosevelt announced he would expand lend-lease orders to the Soviet Union. Hitler's progress there had stalled, and the Nazis were preparing to fight through the winter. Roosevelt felt this was Stalin's chance to regroup. Not everyone was happy with the move. "When we passed that law, it was to aid democracies," an irritated Senator Gerald Nye (R-ND) protested. "Now it is to give Brother Joe one billion smackers with no ifs, no ands, nor buts."[319]

The next day, in a big win for Roosevelt, the Senate passed a revision to the Neutrality Act by a margin of 50–37. The Senate version, however, also permitted merchant ships to visit the port cities of warring nations, which was currently banned under the original Neutrality Act. Roosevelt would now have to wait a week until the House could debate the Senate version.[320] In a vote that was predicted to be a "photo finish," the House narrowly passed the Senate bill by just twelve votes.[321]

Press reports coming from Japan, meanwhile, predicted a "hostile situation" if negotiations with the United States collapsed. Japan had sent an envoy to Washington in what was billed by the Japanese press as a final attempt to make amends. The group was led by Saburō Kurusu, a career diplomat, who used an American football analogy when speaking to reporters in San Francisco. "I fully realize the difficulty of my task," Kurusu stated, "but I hope to break through the line and make a touchdown."

On November 17, 1941, Harry sat down to write what would be his last two letters back home. One was sent to his mother, Eva, and the other to his father, Ralph. In the letter to his mother, Harry finished telling his stories about the time he spent with family in California. Before boarding his ship for Hawaii, Harry had the Fleet Locker Club store several articles of his clothing in moth-proof storage until he returned to Long Beach.[322]

In addition to the word *aloha*, which is Hawaiian for "hello, goodbye, and I love you,"[323] Harry's last words to his mother included a famous English grammatical puzzle. The sentence refers to two students, James and John, who are required by an English teacher to describe a man who had suffered from a cold in the past. The playful Harry, who always had an extremely close relationship with his mother, was eager to see if she could finish the sentence by placing the correct punctuation marks between the words.[324]

Dear Mother,
You're looking at the picture I suppose. Nifty huh! I made them myself from a kit I bought ashore. One may use any negative. The more I make, the better they become. You may have the original snapshot of me on the beach in front of the Royal Hawaiian Hotel.

The first day out to sea after Long Beach (ah what a dear place), mail call sounded and your letter was there. I had mailed my long airmail the night before so knew you hadn't received it yet. There was so much to talk about.....I stretched it to ten pages. I knew you wanted to hear about Great Aunt Minnie and all the folks. My last night ashore I spent with Gene and the folks then saying goodbye to them I walked over to the Hribal's place and visited them for an hour. They had just come home from a Halloween Party at the school...and [I] left at 9:30PM. Fog had come in so dense you could not see more than twenty feet. I called a taxi to take me to my locker club but none was available...so I ran down several blocks until I got one a few minutes later. It was twenty minutes to twelve.....Got to the Fleet Locker Club and did the quickest clothes changing act you ever saw. Ran back out to the desk handing the man a bunch of laundry, asked

him to take care of my clothes and put them in moth proof storage as I might not be back for months. With a—So Long—I sprinted for the dock two blocks away. It was two minutes to twelve when I got there and liberty was up at twelve. Well I need not have hurried as there were a thousand or more sailors... all saying "Goodbye" to their girls, wives, etc. We waited and waited. Finally, one launch came but only 190 men could get in. I waited for the next one as I wanted to stay on "The Good Earth" as long as

Cloth napkin Harry sent to his mother from the Royal Hawaiian Hotel. *Author's collection.*

possible. There is a cafe right there on the docks so Kramer could be seen dashing in every few minutes and devouring a nice big ham sandwich— mmm—with several Coca-Colas on the side. By the time enough boats got there to pick up all those men it was nearly 0200 AM when I stepped on a launch and took one long last look at the beach before it disappeared in the dense fog. Early the same morning we headed out to sea toward a place where pineapple juice and grass skirts are abundant!

I went window shopping in Honolulu and had a lot of fun. It feels so good to get out in the fresh air after being below. It is cooler in the islands now by a few degrees and it sure helps. You should see the Christmas cards I got. They're something different than in the States and I thought the folks would like them.

Can you punctuate the following sentence so it makes good sense?— James while John had had had had had had had had had had had a better effect on the teacher. Try it and give me the answer.

Aloha,

Harry

———

Letter No. 33: Harry Kramer to his father, Ralph Kramer
November 17, 1941
From: Pearl Harbor, Honolulu, HI
To: Chippewa Falls, WI

Ever since Harry first arrived in Hawaii, in April 1940, he had kept up a consistent written correspondence with his mother, Eva. His last letter home was directed to his father, Ralph, in response to a letter that the patriarch had sent to his son. The more serious and reserved Ralph was not known for writing letters, especially since Eva could pass things along that needed to be conveyed. It's extremely likely that recent news stories and global developments had impelled Ralph to write his own letter to Harry.

In response to his father, Harry talked about several casual topics, including the tennis he'd been playing and the reading of *TIME* and *Newsweek* magazines. He also thanked his father for the birthday wishes, in reference to his twenty-second birthday, back on November 10. In a more serious display, Harry let his father know that the government had recently given all sailors a raise. Knowing that his father was still unemployed and looking for gainful work, Harry reminded his father that he could always withdraw whatever funds the family needed from Harry's personal account. With Christmas approaching soon, Harry let his father know that he should use some of his money to purchase his mother a new coat and hat.[325]

On a more emotional note, Harry reminded his father how blessed the family had been since they made the conversion to the Church of Christ, Scientist. Despite Ralph's recent unemployment concerns, they had been healthy and free of any medical debt. Having sensed that his normally stoic father was beginning to worry about Harry's situation as well as the state of the world, Harry wrote, "When I think of all the upheaval and mortal chaos the other people of the world are going through we can certainly be happy and grateful for a lot of things and that there is a constant source of divine power surrounding us at all times from which we may gain help in our problems each day." With those words, Ralph could see how incredible a son he had helped raise. He had grown into a responsible, generous, worldly, patriotic and devout gentleman.[326]

> *Dear Dad,*
>
> *Your letter came on board the last day we were in Long Beach and I got it the next morning at sea. It was so good to read about things back home. I was sorry to learn that the job you wrote for did not materialize but I'm proud that you received a mark anyway....We know that things will work out in Divine Law. I often think of the things we have to be thankful for even though the employment problems seem to be hard to overcome. None of us have ever been sick and there has been no doctor bills to take care of since we've been in the Church of Christ Science. When I think of all the upheaval and mortal chaos the people of the world are going through we can certainly be happy and grateful for a lot of things and that there is a constant source of divine power surrounding us at all times from which we may gain help in our problems each day. Dad, anytime you need something like your license plates or get anything for dear mother you just go to the bank and draw what you need, then later on you may write and tell me about it. I'm glad I have some money in reserve like that and don't ever feel backward about using some to help out. I'll be very happy if mother can have a nice coat. If you'd like to get her a nice hat to match, go ahead and draw out enough for that too.*
>
> *I have some good news. Congress has passed a bill authorizing a ten dollar raise for all hands. It has only one place to go through in the naval bureau before it becomes effective so we all believe it is almost a certain thing and we get all the back pay from August 19th. That will help a lot and $120 a year extra will pay all my insurance, etc. Are you getting that twenty dollar allotment regularly each month now? I spent part of my funds*

I had saved up on the books for my recreation period in Long Beach and now building it back up again.

I played tennis the other evening and had a good time. It sure is wonderful to get out and enjoy some fresh air once in a while. Being down below I feel sort of tired out from not staying out in the open.

Do you ever get to read "Time" or "Newsweek" magazines? I read them quite often and find them very interesting. They are a big help in providing me with a complete news picture of world events.

Thanks for the swell birthday cards. I surely will know how to clean out the barracks now!

Aloha,
Harry

PART III

The First Boy Killed
from Chippewa County

Chapter 1

UNEASY PEACE

On November 27, 1941, Japan's diplomatic envoy arrived in D.C. Both the Japanese and American press foresaw the mission as one rooted in eventual failure, as the two sides remained far apart. A day prior to Roosevelt's meeting with the envoy, Secretary of State Cordell Hull was instructed to give the United States' final offer to Japan. Officially titled the "Outline of Proposed Basis for Agreement Between the United States and Japan," the document became known as the Hull Note. It was based on a list of ten steps to be mutually taken. The United States called for Japan to withdraw from China and French Indochina, in exchange for negotiations leading to improved trade and economic status. To ease concerns about potential American expansionism, the United States agreed waive any extraterritorial claims in the region.[327]

Japanese news agencies largely denounced the proposals as a sign of disrespect for Japan's autonomy in the Far East. Rather than denounce the outline, Japan provided no response. Letting actions speak louder than words, Japan moved additional military forces into French Indochina, causing the Roosevelt administration to speculate that an invasion of Thailand was imminent. Further diplomatic "discussions were in abeyance" until Japanese leaders processed the details in the so-called Hull Note. Japanese officials did assure the United States that their recent buildup near Thailand was simply "precautionary" and not a sign of aggression.[328] An uneasy Roosevelt waited for Japan's response, as American officials feared an attack on Thailand would springboard to Singapore, the Dutch East Indies or the Philippines.[329] Two days later, on December 6, the *Chippewa Herald-Telegram* ran the headline "Uneasy Peace Strains Pacific Tension While US Waits Japan's Moves."[330]

Chapter 2

A DAY OF INFAMY

Decexecember 7, 1941, began as a normal Sunday in Hawaii. The weather service marked sunrise at 6:26 a.m. and predicted a morning low temperature of 70 degrees, with an afternoon high of 78. A forecast of mild winds, "partially cloudy" skies and "good visibility" promised an exceptional day for all sailors, both on and off ship.[331] The *California* was one of seven battleships moored in the harbor, with an eighth sitting in dry dock across the channel. Unlike neighboring *Maryland*, *Oklahoma*, *Tennessee*, *West Virginia*, *Arizona* and *Nevada*, *California* was moored alone at the southern tip of "Battleship Row." In total, 102 vessels were in the harbor, including cruisers, destroyers, submarines, minesweepers and other craft and service ships.[332]

It being Sunday, the right-side deck of the *California*'s bow, or starboard forecastle, had been rigged with a large canopy to provide cover for the day's church services. Catholic chaplain William Maguire was to board the ship at eight o'clock, hear confessions at eight thirty and perform a full Catholic service at nine. At ten, a Protestant service would be held for the rest. Later that evening, movies were to be shown on the quarterdeck, beginning at seven thirty.[333] All in all, sailors looked forward to Sundays, as they were normally free of surprise drills.

The one major caveat to the *California*'s status was that the ship was set to undergo a major material inspection the following day. In preparation, "Condition X-Ray" had been ordered the night before, which meant that the ship was presumed to be in little danger of attack or natural hazards.

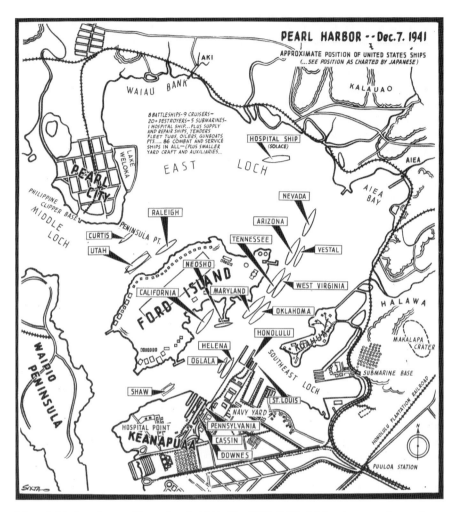

Map of ship locations on December 7, 1941. The USS *California*'s berth was at the southern tip of Battleship Row, just off the eastern side of Ford Island, circa 1941. *U.S. Navy.*

As a result, the crew opened "certain manhole covers on voids," located on the third deck, for "inspection and maintenance" purposes. With third deck currently situated five feet below the ship's current draft water line, any unexpected surge of water would cause serious flooding belowdecks.[334] When properly closed and in place, these covers maintained the watertight status of key compartments within the bowels of the ship, preventing water from the upper decks from flooding into the lower ones. In addition, other portholes and exterior doors were also opened. Luckily for the crew, the peaceful confines of Pearl Harbor afforded the ideal backdrop for an inspection of this sort.[335]

At approximately 7:55 a.m., as Chaplain Maguire patiently awaited his transport, Japanese aircraft began their coordinated surprise. Launched from four heavy aircraft carriers, located some 230 miles northwest of the island of Oahu, a total of 353 aircraft attacked the naval base in two distinct waves. The force included "40 torpedo planes, 103 level bombers, 131 dive-bombers, and 79 fighters." Supporting these carrier-based groups were two Japanese "heavy cruisers, two light cruisers, thirty-five submarines, two battleships, and eleven destroyers." Over the course of the next one hour and fifteen minutes, the attack killed a staggering "2,403 US personnel, including 68 civilians" and left another 1,178 wounded. While the U.S. Pacific Fleet's entire complement of aircraft carriers (3) had been spared, as they were out on maneuvers, the Japanese had destroyed or damaged 19 U.S. Navy ships, including 8 battleships. On the battleship USS *Arizona* alone, 1,177 sailors were killed. A whopping 169 American aircraft were also destroyed, with another 159 damaged. The aircraft had been proactively grouped in clumps, to dissuade acts of sabotage on the ground, and this arrangement left them vulnerable to aerial assaults. For its part, in the attack, Japan lost a total of 29 aircraft, 5 midget submarines and 129 soldiers.[336] December 7, 1941, would go down as one of the most devastating military events in American history.

The next day, Roosevelt addressed the nation in a joint session of Congress in the United States Capitol. The speech lasted only six and a half minutes, and it was best remembered for its opening line: "Yesterday, December 7, 1941—a date which will live in infamy—the United States of America was suddenly and deliberately attacked by naval and air forces of the Empire of Japan." Heard on the radio by an estimated 81 percent of the country, the president called on Americans to mobilize and for Congress to send him an official declaration of war. Both the House, 388–1, and the Senate, 82–0, approved the measure. Later that day, 4:10 p.m., Roosevelt signed the war declaration into law. The United States was officially at war with Japan.[337]

Chapter 3

TRAGEDY ABOARD USS *CALIFORNIA*

Within the larger attack that encompassed Pearl Harbor Naval Station, each specific location on base had its own unique experience that day. The *California* began the morning in a vulnerable position. Preparations for the following day's inspection had left the ship's watertight status in doubt, while limiting its defenses to just two 5-inch guns, with fifty shells, and two .50-caliber machine guns, with four hundred rounds. Additionally, neither of the ship's top two officers, Captain J.W. Bunkley and Executive Officer E.E. Stone, were on board, as each was in Honolulu for business. Leadership responsibilities fell to Lieutenant Commander M.N. Little.[338]

Just after 7:55 a.m., the resonating sounds of explosions rang throughout the harbor. Just before 8:00, the *California*'s loudspeaker blared the words "Air raid! Air raid!" with an immediate call for all men to get to their assigned general quarters, or battle stations. Lieutenant Commander Little urgently ordered the ship into material conditions YOKE and ZED, thus shifting the *California* into a watertight war footing. The ship's personnel, bravely and frantically, raced to their battle stations as more Japanese airplanes wreaked havoc. By 8:03, the two readied machine gun positions fired at Japanese torpedo planes as they made their final approach toward the ship. At 8:05, two torpedo blasts near simultaneously struck the port, or left side, of the ship. The first detonated in the forward (or front) section, creating a twenty-four-foot-long hole below the protective armor belt. This led to instantaneous flooding of compartments on the third deck, due to the open covers. It also ruptured the fuel oil tanks, which caused their contents to either spill loose or get contaminated by the salt water. The noxious fuel oil and seawater mixture infiltrated the ship's unsecured ventilation system, causing it to spread quickly and forcing the men to evacuate numerous compartments below decks.[339]

A second torpedo, which hit the aft, or rear, section of the ship, inflicted a forty-foot-long hole beneath the ship's protective armor belt. Once again, water rushed through open manholes on the third deck, causing flooding in and evacuations from the voids beneath them. Within minutes, the crew was ordered to begin counterflooding on the ship's starboard, or right, side as the *California* begin to list dangerously to its left. The hope was to reduce *California's* ominous list, to prevent the ship from capsizing onto its side. Just as crews began firing the ship's two 5-inch guns at approaching Japanese dive-bombers, at approximately 8:10 a.m., the entire ship lost all its lights and engine power, due to salt water infiltrating the power plant's fuel oil supply. At 8:20, the powerless *California* was shocked by vibrations from a near-miss aerial bomb near the portside bow. This flooded several more forward compartments, which forced the head of the ship down by three and a half feet. By 8:25, four additional bombs were observed being dropped near the *California* off the starboard side. Each caused various amounts of near-miss damage.[340]

In the midst of the escalating chaos, machine gunners aboard *California* shot down at least two enemy aircraft, including a Japanese dive-bomber. Then, at approximately eighty forty-five, the *California* suffered its most significant blow. An aerial bomber dropped a 551-pound munition that struck the "upper deck at frame 59, about 7 feet inboard from the starboard," or right, side of the ship. It "penetrated the main deck and ricocheted from the second deck inboard and exploded (in A-611), blowing a large hole in the main deck above (in A-705)."[341] The damage inflicted was catastrophic, including a minimum of 50 men killed, many others wounded and a massive series of fires spreading across multiple decks.[342]

By 9:00 a.m., power and lighting had been restored, and Captain Bunkley and Executive Officer Stone had returned to the ship. With the Japanese attack seemingly over by 9:20, the *California's* crew set about rescuing men, putting out fires and continuing the counterflooding measures to reduce the listing. Due to reports of fuel oil flames approaching atop surface water, Captain Bunkley temporarily ordered the crew to abandon ship. Thirteen minutes later, at 10:15, the order was canceled, and the crew returned to the *California*. But, with no feasible way to prevent water from entering the

The listing USS *California*, shown with a white canopy set up for Sunday church services, would eventually settle and rest on the harbor floor, 1941. *U.S. Navy.*

ship, the counterflooding measures simply made the ship sink deeper into the harbor. The ship was eventually abandoned, this time for good. In the coming days, the *California* would not only come to rest at the bottom of the forty-foot harbor but also sink an additional sixteen feet into the mud.[343] Six days later, with the *California* officially sunk, Captain Bunkley summarized the damage in his log: "37 dead have been positively identified. There are still 116 men missing." The full extent of the loss of life would not be realized until salvage and recovery operations reached completion in April 1942. A total of 103 servicemen died from the USS *California*.[344]

Chapter 4

UNBEARABLE GRIEF

The first wave of information regarding the attack reached Chippewa Falls through radio broadcasts, telegrams and phone calls. When Ralph and Eva Kramer first heard that Pearl Harbor had been attacked, the couple immediately drove to visit their eldest son, Robert. Like other Americans, the Kramers were in complete shock. Radio reports were vague and focused on the attack from a wider purview. Ralph, Eva, Robert and Marie wanted to know only one thing: Was Harry OK?

The *Chippewa Herald-Telegram*, which didn't publish on Sundays, broke the story in its Monday edition with the headline: "US Declares War on Japan." News released by the White House claimed at least two battleships had been sunk, four destroyers damaged and a large number of planes destroyed. They also predicted that the total casualties would balloon well past three thousand, with over half of them fatalities. As the Kramers pored through the Monday newspaper, they saw it included a predictive battle map illustrating how the United States and the Soviet Union could partner together to retaliate against Japan. Titled "Pacific Picture: A Dark One for Japan—She Painted It," including probable navy attack lanes and potential aircraft striking locations in Alaska and the Philippines. In an article titled "Japan Gambles on All-Out War with US," it was made known to the American people that the attack on Pearl Harbor had inflicted "heavy damage" but that the heart of the Pacific Fleet was very much intact. But there was no word on Harry or the *California*.[345]

Ralph and Eva were starved for news about their son and his ship. On December 8, the *Chippewa Herald-Telegram* printed a battleship graphic listing the *Arizona*, *West Virginia* and *Oklahoma* as having been "sunk," while another unnamed vessel had been labeled as "lost." The navy still hadn't released any information on that one.[346]

Finally, on the morning of December 16, nine days after the attack and nine days before Christmas, Ralph and Eva finally received word. A courier from the Western Union Company arrived to deliver the following message:

> *Ralph B. Kramer*
> *21 Well Street*
> *Chippewa Falls, WI.*
>
>
>
> > *The Navy Department deeply regrets to inform you that your son Harry Wellington Kramer, Fireman First Class, United States Navy, was lost in action in the performance of his duty and in service of his country. The department extends to you its sincerest sympathy in your great loss. To prevent possible aid to our enemies please do not divulge the name of his ship or station. If remains are recovered they will be interred temporarily in the locality where death occurred and you will be notified accordingly.*
> > *Rear Admiral C. W. Nimitz*
> > *Chief of the Bureau of Navigation*[347]

The news about Harry left Ralph and Eva, now aged fifty-seven and sixty-two, devastated. While it had never been verbalized, it had always been perceived by friends and family that Harry was the couple's favorite son. Like his father, Harry possessed an infectious charisma, an innate urge for travel and adventure and a natural relatability that endeared him to friend and stranger alike. Reflecting his mother, Harry was gentle, soft-spoken and deeply rooted in the tenets of the Christian Science faith. Conversely, Harry seemed devoid of his father's occasional bombastic and domineering tendencies. Nor did he reflect his mother's noticeable meekness or her overly obedient persona. Harry was academically motivated, diversely intelligent and seemed to be gifted with the most prized attributes of both parents. While their eldest son was close to—and deeply loved and respected by—his parents, it was Harry who had brought an extra twinkle to their eyes. He was the son who seemed best positioned to transcend the family's economic hardships of Great Depression–era Wisconsin. Now, at the age of twenty-two, Harry was gone.[348]

A Kramer family photo taken just months after Harry's death in 1942. *Back row*: Harry's father, Ralph; his mother, Eva, holding his niece, Evelyne; his grandmother Ualia Webb, Elsie Grip, Anton Grip and Harry's older brother, Robert. First row: Harry's nephews David, Gerald, Carl and Earl. *Author's collection.*

The Kramers tried their best to process the shocking, horrific and unceremonious news of Harry's death. At age eighty-five, Ualia lost her beloved grandson. Robert, now thirty, was robbed of a younger brother he admired and adored. Marie, while in the final days of the couple's fifth pregnancy, tried to manage the enthusiasm she felt for the child's arrival with the anguish of having lost her brother-in-law. On December 19, Marie gave birth to the couple's first daughter, Evelyne Marie Kramer. Her arrival ended up being a godsend, as she was perceived as a much-needed light in the family's sea of darkness. For Ralph and Eva, the arrival of their first granddaughter was especially meaningful.[349]

Complicating the family's grieving was the notoriety Harry's death received. He wasn't just their loss but the entire community's. On the same day the telegram was received, his death made front page news: "Harry Kramer Is Japanese Raid Victim." The paper identified their son as the "First Chippewa County Boy to Give Life for Country." In neighboring Eau Claire, the place of Harry's birth, the *Leader-Telegram* declared, "Chippewa Youth Killed in Action."[350] While several other Chippewa Falls boys had been stationed at Pearl Harbor that day, including James Doucette, Tom Carroll, Roland Forrester, Phillip Anderson, Robert Boudreau and brothers

Claude and David P. Bergeron, all had survived the attack.[351] There was still no word on Earl White, Harry's classmate, who was stationed on the capsized USS *Oklahoma*. In total, fifty-six servicemen from Wisconsin died at Pearl Harbor, including five aboard the USS *California* battleship.[352]

From these front-page headlines, news of Harry's death quickly spread throughout Chippewa Falls and western Wisconsin. The Kramer family was inundated with condolences and warm wishes. Words of comfort arrived from the Kramers' Church of Christ, Science, while messages of patriotic consolation were received from the Chippewa Falls American Legion and Veterans of Foreign Wars organizations. On December 20, the *Chippewa Herald-Telegram* published a poem that paid tribute to Harry and the rest of the Pearl Harbor victims. It read:

> *Remember the boys who sailed out of the Bay, remember the ones who returned not that day.*
> *Remember the part that we have to play, and never forget Pearl Harbor.*
> *Never forget them—the boys good and true, the boys who defended the Red, White, and Blue.*
> *That we may be safe in our own happy land, so it's shoulder to shoulder that we have to stand.*
> *And Remember Pearl Harbor.*
> *Let not the enemy surprise us again, let's keep the flag flying afloat, and ashore, that freedom be ours now and ever more.*
> *And always Remember Pearl Harbor*
> *Dedicated to Harry Kramer* [353]

Harry's two closest friends also took the news hard. Jack Selden, who exchanged numerous letters with Harry, was crushed. His younger sister Jean, then age six, recalled how everyone in the home was in complete shock and disbelief. Jack, now age sixteen, had lost one of his dearest friends and older mentors.

Mortimer Anderson, Harry's best friend, heard the news while stationed at Kessler Field in Mississippi. Serving as a military policeman in the Army Air Corps, the twenty-two-year-old wrote a letter to Harry's father on December 23:

> *Mr. Kramer,*
> *I don't know how or what to say but I'd like to have been home when you got that bad news. I probably could have been some assistance. It really*

Left: Jack Selden joined the U.S. Navy after graduation, partially motivated to avenge Harry's death, circa 1945. *Author's collection.*

Right: Chippewa Falls High School students fundraise for the war effort, 1943. *Author's collection.*

hit me hard to hear that the best friend I had got killed in action. He was more than a friend, he was like a brother. How's grandma and the rest of the family?

I had been writing to Harry about every other week and I didn't get any answers for the past three months.

Say, I wish you and the rest of the family the best of luck and a Merry, Merry Christmas and a Happy New Year…

Keep your chin up.

Love,

Mort "Your Other Boy" [354]

As the holiday season came and went, Ralph and Eva were still in disbelief. They had so many unanswered questions, yet no one to provide any answers. Are they sure it was him? Is it possible this was all a mistake? How did he die? Did he suffer? Where was he found? Deep down, the couple held out hope that another letter would arrive, this time from Harry, saying it was all a big misunderstanding. Then, on January 6, 1942, a letter arrived from Harry's captain, J.W. Bunkley. It stated:

> *Dear Mr. Kramer (Ralph),*
>
> *It is with a feeling of deepest regret that I must now address you to report the death of your son, resulting from enemy action, at Pearl Harbor, on December seventh.*
>
> *I wish to convey to you my sincere sympathy and condolences. Harry Kramer was a man of splendid character, who did his duty in this most critical time with unflinching courage and gallantry.*
>
> *Be assured that his memory will be an inspiration to us who remain to carry on, that his and your sacrifices were not in vain, but will renew our determination to keep our country safe from all enemies.*
>
> *Sincerely,*
> *J.W. Bunkley*
> *Captain, USS California, US Navy*[355]

Eight days later, on January 14, the information contained in Captain Bunkley's letter was reaffirmed by Frank Knox, President Franklin Roosevelt's secretary of the navy. It stated:

> *My Dear Mr. Kramer (Ralph),*
>
> *I desire to offer you my personal condolence in the tragic death of your son, Harry Wellington Kramer, Fireman First Class, United States Navy, which occurred at the time of the attack by the Japanese on December seventh.*
>
> *It is hoped that you may find comfort in the thought that he made the supreme sacrifice upholding the highest traditions of the Navy, in defense of his country.*
>
> *Very Sincerely Yours,*
> *Frank Knox*
> *Secretary of the Navy*[356]

Harry was indeed dead. In the coming months, Harry's name would be invoked to galvanize Chippewa Valley residents to support the nation's war mobilization, including bond drives organized by the city's schoolchildren and the enlistment of dozens of area men into the ranks of the armed forces. But, despite the support and tributes Ralph and Eva had received, the pain associated with Harry's death would never subside. For the rest of their lives, Ralph and Eva shied away from celebrating Christmas. More noticeably, they avoided publicly conversing about Harry, including with their family and closest friends.[357]

Chapter 5

AGONY IN THE UNKNOWN

On December 11, four days after the attack, Captain J.W. Bunkley used the ship's logbook to document the names, service numbers and ranks of the "37 known dead," "70 wounded" and "116 still missing." The sixteenth name in the alphabetical list of the dead was "Kramer, H.W., 328-65-18, F1C." No specific information pertaining to cause and location of death was provided, not for Harry nor any other sailor. Was Harry's body found and physically identified? Did someone on board witness him dying? Or was he simply presumed dead, based on his last known location on board the ship?[358] The initial death notice telegram, sent by Rear Admiral Nimitz, revealed an unfortunate ambiguity: "If remains are recovered they will be interred temporarily in the locality where death occurred and you will be notified accordingly." Was the phrase "if remains are recovered" standard U.S. Navy phraseology for such a telegram? Or was his body not found yet? Lastly, how long would the family have to wait until they would be "notified accordingly"?[359]

Ralph and Eva would endure years of agony as they waited for correspondences that might never come. All they could do was speculate as to which horrific scenario cost their dear son his life. According to Harry's letters, his last known assignment was in the freshwater hold. His last known battle station was beneath turret no. 2. If he was in either of those two locations, then he was deep within the bowels of the ship. In that case, the front torpedo hit and the devastating bomb were the likely culprits. Had

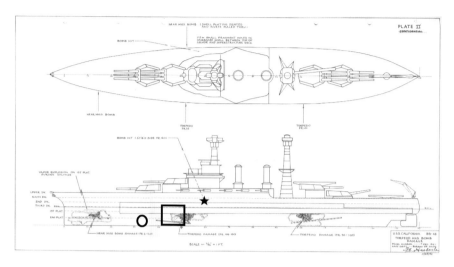

The location of the devastating second bomb blast (*star*), which caused extensive immediate and secondary damage, was in direct proximity to Harry's last known battle station assignment in the handling room (*rectangle*). His last known daily workstation was near the freshwater hold (*small circle*). *Author's collection.*

Harry been anywhere near those two locations, he could have experienced deadly fires, catastrophic explosions, lethal air contamination and/or rapid flooding that could have led to drowning.

On the off chance Harry was able to physically evacuate the ship, he could have faced a dangerous mix of burning surface oil in the harbor's water, which had been floating toward the *California* from other wounded vessels in Battleship Row. All options were plausible. Contemplating any of them was heart-wrenching. To talk about Harry, regardless of the topic, always seemed to segue into more painful questions, speculation and theories about his death.

Throughout all their confusion and heartache, Ralph and Eva forged ahead and supported the war effort as best as they knew how. To the press, they remained stoic and patriotic when asked about Harry. Like so many other Americans did, the couple scraped together their extra money to purchase war bonds. In a very personal gesture, designed to benefit Harry's fellow servicemen, they donated all their son's books to the Chippewa Falls chapter of the Victory Book campaign. As "Harry Kramer will never again spend a quiet evening paging through his favorite books in the comfort of his home in Chippewa Falls," the *Milwaukee Journal Sentinel* newspaper wrote, "his books…will go out into the army and marine camps, or perhaps the ships of the navy, to help lighten the hours of Harry's erstwhile fighting mates."[360]

As the months passed by, Ralph, Eva and Robert hoped more details would surface. Periodically, letters or packages would arrive in the mail related to their fallen son. An envelope from the White House was received, which contained a small poster signed by Franklin Roosevelt. The president, a navy veteran himself, inscribed it with the message, "In memory of Harry." In July 1942, after *California* had been raised and salvaged, a package purportedly containing Harry's personal effects were mailed home. They included an American flag and two uniform patches, or chevrons. Did that flag drape Harry's casket? Did they find his body? Neither patch reflected Harry's rank, as one indicated water tender first class and the other water tender second class. Did the navy incorrectly mail someone else's things? Or did Harry collect them from other sailors as they advanced through the ranks or discarded them? Once again, only more questions and few answers.[361]

In March 1943, the American Legion sent Ralph and Eva an official "Gold Star Citation," recognizing them as having made the ultimate sacrifice to their country. The citation honored Harry's service by acknowledging that "this death occurred in order that others might live." To symbolize the Kramers' loss, the group included a personal-sized "Gold Star Flag" that featured a gold star set on a white background and finished with red framing.[362] Later that year, in December, the Navy Department mailed the Kramers Harry's Purple Heart citation and medal. The citation read, "For Military Merit and for Wounds Received in Action Resulting in His Death, December 7, 1941."[363] While Ralph and Eva were both honored and appreciative of the acknowledgements, what they really wanted was more answers. When was the navy going to provide them with an update, as promised back in its initial telegram?

As the years passed, so, too, did the world war that had raged across the globe. The United States and its allies defeated the Axis powers in 1945. Victory in Europe, or VE Day, came on May 8, while Victory over Japan, or VJ Day, was achieved on August 14. Conservative estimates place the human loss at 15 million battle deaths, 25 million wounded and 45 million civilian deaths. Of that total, the United States had 416,800 military-related deaths, including those inflicted at Pearl Harbor.[364] Ralph and Eva, along with other Americans, would read about war developments and battles such as D-Day, the Battle of the Bulge, Okinawa and Iwo Jima. They would learn about the unfathomable atrocities and genocide carried out by Hitler and his

Left: Harry's Purple Heart (*front*), 1943. *Author's collection.*

Right: Harry's Purple Heart (*reverse*), 1943. *Author's collection.*

ilk, as his Holocaust deliberately murdered upward of 6 million Jews and an additional 5 million other people deemed undesirables.[365]

Ralph and Eva would also witness the United States develop into the world's first atomic superpower. As President Harry Truman weighed his options for defeating a defiant Japan, Roosevelt's former vice president was alarmed by the casualty estimates connected to an all-out American invasion of the Japanese mainland. As a safer alternative for American servicemen, on August 6, 1945, the United States dropped its first atomic bomb on the city of Hiroshima, instantly killing around eighty thousand Japanese. Three days later, after Japan's refusal to surrender, a second bomb was dropped on Nagasaki, instantly killing another forty thousand. Over the coming years, tens of thousands of additional Japanese citizens would die from radiation-related ailments and illnesses.[366]

Upon the conclusion of the war, Congress allocated funds to construct a new and permanent national military cemetery in Honolulu. After the attack, the dead from the USS *California* had been interred in temporary cemeteries named Halawa and Nu'uanu. White wooden crosses marked each grave, either with the serviceman's name or the word "unknown." Of the 103 interments from *California*, only 42 were initially buried as "known remains." Each victim was buried in their own individual grave, unlike the mass graves of those from the *Oklahoma*.[367]

In 1947, nearly six years after the attack, the military began the painstaking task of exhuming the graves, for the purposes of identifying or confirming the identities of each. As the process played out, individual corpses were stored in Mausoleum No. 2 at Schofield Barracks. After examination, each would then be reinterred in the soon-to-be-opened National Memorial Cemetery of the Pacific. It was nicknamed the Punchbowl, as it was set in a volcanic crater overlooking the city of Honolulu.

In January 1949, over eight years after the attack at Pearl Harbor, Ralph and Eva finally received some answers pertaining to their son. Rear admiral and U.S. Navy surgeon general C.A. Swanson wrote:

Dear Mr. Kramer,

It is with deep regret that I inform you that the remains of "Unknown X-104," interred in the Halawa Naval Cemetery, Oahu, Territory of Hawaii, Grave 661 in Plot C, have been identified as those of your son, Harry Wellington Kramer, Fireman First Class, US Navy. These remains were recovered from the USS California following the Japanese attack on Pearl Harbor on December 7, 1941, but identification could not be made at that time and they were buried as unidentified. The remains were recently exhumed and processed by a specially trained identification unit, and identity was established by comparison of dental and physical characteristics with the dental record and physical description of your son.

Enclosed with this letter are two pamphlets relating to disposition of the remains of World War II dead. An application form upon which you are requested to express your wishes for final interment of your son's remains is also enclosed.

Before completing, it is requested that you read carefully the pamphlets of information regarding the return of the dead. After you have read them carefully and have made your decision, please execute the application form and return it immediately in the accompanying envelope which requires no postage, as your son's remains are being held above ground pending receipt of instruction for disposition. If you desire to delegate authority to claim the remains to some other person, who has agreed to assume this

responsibility, please execute Part II of the application form and return it in the enclosed envelope without delay.
Sincerely yours,
C.A. Swanson
Rear Admiral
Surgeon General, US Navy[368]

The identification of Harry's physical remains was done by utilizing his physical examination files, including information about his height and weight, one missing tooth and the distinctive overbite that nearly prevented his enlistment. Even though the specific cause of death was not known, Ralph, Eva and Robert could at least take comfort that Harry had been found. For reasons unknown, the couple elected to have their son's remains stay in Hawaii. It may have been because they wanted to keep Harry with his fellow crew members or because they knew how much Harry had fallen in love with Waikiki and Nanakuli. Given their sensitivity and pain at the mere discussion of their son, maybe it was just easier to think of Harry as being "away," as if he was still off on his adventure.

The Kramers received their final correspondence concerning Harry's death in November 1952. Colonel James Clearwater mailed the couple information about, and a photograph of, Harry's final gravesite. He wrote:

Dear Mr. Kramer
A photograph of the grave of your loved one, Fireman First Class Harry Wellington Kramer, 328-65-18, in the National Memorial Cemetery of the Pacific, Honolulu (Section F, Plot 675), Territory of Hawaii, and a descriptive folder containing a brief history of the cemetery are enclosed.
The National Memorial Cemetery of the Pacific is one of the most beautiful of our national cemeteries. Provision has been made to assure that it will be maintained and cared for in a manner befitting the last resting place of our honored dead.
These small tokens are sent as evidence of the respect and gratitude of your government for the sacrifices made by the members of the armed forces and their families.
Sincerely yours,
James B. Clearwater
Colonel, QMC
Chief, Memorial Division[369]

At long last, Ralph and Eva, and their eldest son, Robert, could feel some semblance of peace.

AFTERWORD

Harry Wellington Kramer's life and death inspired countless individuals to participate in, or contribute to, the greatest and most efficient war mobilization in American history. Schoolchildren collected money to purchase bonds, while hundreds of Chippewa Falls high school graduates, from numerous graduating classes, either enlisted in or were drafted into the country's military ranks. At least twenty-eight men who attended Chippewa Falls public schools, including Harry, died while serving in World War II. Many had their physical remains interred in unfamiliar land, far from their native Chippewa Falls.[370] Two of those men, Robert E. Baldeshwiler (who died at Saipan in 1944)[371] and Desmond G. Kurth (who died at Iwo Jima in 1945),[372] are buried near Harry in the National Memorial Cemetery of the Pacific in Honolulu, Hawaii.

Harry's ship, USS *California*, would live to fight another day. After salvage efforts were completed and the ship was made seaworthy, the "Prune Barge" was carefully floated back to the Puget Sound Navy Yards, in Bremerton, for refurbishment. Once it was completed, in January 1944, it quickly joined the Pacific Fleet in East Asia. The *California* participated in numerous engagements and fought in the Battles of Leyte Gulf and Lingayen Gulf. During the latter, it was hit by a Japanese kamikaze pilot, killing 44 sailors and injuring an additional 155. After the war, *California* was decommissioned, and it was sold for scrap in 1959. Today, the ship's 350-pound cast bronze bell is on display at the California State Capitol Park in Sacramento.[373]

Plot Map of
The National Memorial Cemetery of the Pacific

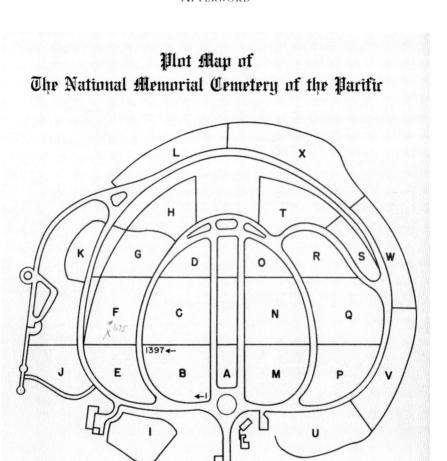

Sections are lettered as shown and graves are numbered in each plot in numerical sequence beginning with one in the corner nearest the flag pole and then in order to the far corner of the plot (See Plot B for example).

The Office and Restrooms are located near the flag pole.

Derived from the Hawaiian word *Pūowaina*, meaning "hill of sacrifice," Punchbowl Crater is an extinct volcanic tuff cone now transformed into one of America's most hallowed military cemeteries. Over fifty-three thousand veterans and their eligible relatives are now here. The three Chippewa Falls World War II casualties buried here are Harry Kramer (Plot F 675), Desmond Kurth (Plot E 656) and Robert Baldeshwiler (Plot B 878). *Find a Grave.*

The USS *California* (*left*) resting on the seafloor of Pearl Harbor, 1942. She would be salvaged, repaired, refurbished and fight again within the U.S. Pacific Fleet. *U.S. Navy.*

As for the 103 crewmembers killed aboard *California*, the fates of 20 sailors remain unresolved today. According to the military's Defense POW/MIA Accounting Agency, 42 of the victims had been initially buried as "known," while the rest were interred individually as "unknown." During the mass disinterment in 1947, dog tags, medical records and physical descriptions were used to identify another 40 men, including Harry. Today, the National Memorial Cemetery of the Pacific contains the remains of 25 unknown men the agency believes are "potentially associated" with *California*. During the chaotic attack, men from other ships were in *California*'s vicinity, thus complicating the identification process. Modern-day DNA testing has been used to solve several of these cases, but not every family had submitted a comparative sample.[374]

Tragically, Harry wasn't the only Chippewa Valley sailor to be buried as "unidentified" following the attack at Pearl Harbor. Frank E. Nicoles, Harry's fellow naval enlistee, was also killed. Stationed aboard the battleship USS *Oklahoma*, Nicoles had also risen to the rank of fireman first class. He was one of 429 crewmen who died aboard *Oklahoma* that day. Some seventy-four years after his death, on May 5, 2016, Nicoles's remains were positively identified, and they were reinterred in a military cemetery, near surviving relatives, in San Antonio, Texas.[375] While Harry Kramer is recognized as the first World War II casualty from Chippewa County, Nicoles was the first from neighboring Eau Claire County.[376] While it's unknown if the two men ever met in life, they are now indelibly linked by their place in area history.

As for the people Harry wrote about in his letters, each kept his memory close to their heart and continued to live their lives. Hart Wood Sr., the Hawaiian-based architect, would witness three of his four sons serve in the war. In August 1944, one of Hart and Jessie Wood's sons, First Lieutenant Thomas L. Wood, died after his plane was shot down over France.[377]

Great Aunt "Minnie" Durfee, who had been so gracious and welcoming, passed away in 1951, at the age of ninety—but not before she lost her own son. Just nineteen days after Harry's death, acclaimed architect Morien Durfee Sr. succumbed to eye cancer, after it metastasized into his liver and lungs.[378] Minnie's daughter Ruth died in 1983 at the age of ninety-four.[379]

Harry's two distant cousins experienced drastically divergent fates. Morien Durfee Jr., whose extensive record collection inspired Harry to start his own, died from polio in 1943. He was just twenty-two. Glen Liddiard, who gave Harry his first and only airplane ride, went on to have a notable career at the Navy Electronics Laboratory (NEL). There he assisted in the "design, procurement, testing, installation and maintenance of electronic equipment for the US Navy."[380] Glen and his wife had two children, Don and Carol, and lived in Southern California until his passing in 2009, at age eighty-nine.[381]

The other notable family Harry spent time with was that of Theodore and Alice Marie Hribal. Alice Marie passed away in 1957, at the rather young age of fifty-four, while Theodore lived to be seventy-four. Both of their daughters, Hope and Alice Theresa, went on to earn doctoral degrees. During the war, Hope worked as a naval shipyard electrician, and she later became the medical director of a health center in San Francisco. Dr. Hope Corey died in 1983, at the age of fifty-seven.[382] Her younger sister Alice Marie, who had impressed Harry with her math and Spanish skills, became a professor at the California School of Chiropody, also in San Francisco. Dr. Alice Theresa Dodge passed away in 2005, at age seventy-eight.[383]

While all of Harry's friends and family would come to learn about his death at Pearl Harbor, it's not known if Mildred Grant ever learned of the news herself. After first meeting Harry in a reading room in Seattle, the elder widow was constantly on the move. Her life's journey spanned Wisconsin, Idaho, Oregon, Washington, California and New York. Her last stop was New York City, and she died there in 1968 at age seventy-eight.[384]

All the classmates Harry wrote about survived the war. After the navy, Jack Larson returned to his native Lancaster, Wisconsin, got married, raised three kids and worked as an insurance salesman. He passed away in 2012 at age ninety-one.[385] Loyal Lubach, who served in the U.S. Army Air Corps, became a successful businessman in California. After he and his wife raised their four children, they returned to Chippewa Falls. He died there in 1981 at the age of eighty-nine.[386] Benjamin "Benny" Smith returned to the Chippewa Valley after his military service. He, too, married after the war and had three children. He worked as a maintenance man for the Eau Claire School District and passed away in 1979, at the age of sixty.[387] Earl White, who served aboard the USS *Oklahoma*, survived the attack that killed Frank E. Nicoles and so many others. Earl returned to Chippewa Falls and got a job working with the developmentally disabled. He passed away in 2002 at the age of eighty-two.[388] Mortimer Anderson, Harry's best friend, remained in Mississippi after his marriage. He and his wife raised two children in Gulfport, where Mort worked as a chiropractor under the name Dr. M.C. Anderson. He died in 1986, at age sixty-seven.[389]

Having never gotten over the loss of his dear friend, Jack Selden promptly joined the navy after high school graduation. He served in both World War II and Korea and finished his career working in military intelligence. Jack was credited with having worked as a project manager for the United States' ballistic missile early warning system. His life's professional work was predicated on making sure that what happened to Harry would not be replicated. Leaving behind a wife and two daughters, Jack died in 1990, at the age of sixty-four.

Jack's younger sister, Jean Selden, still resides in Chippewa Falls. Born in 1934, she was just seven years old when Pearl Harbor was attacked. She remembers Harry as a tall, friendly, courteous and nice-looking young man who was a very close friend of her brother's. Jean would go on to marry and raise a family of her own, including two children, Bruce and Dawn.[390]

Through the duration of the war years, Ralph and Eva Kramer continued to live at 21 Well Street. On June 9, 1945, Harry's beloved maternal grandmother, Ualia Webb, passed away at the age of eighty-eight.[391] Her death left Ralph and Eva alone in their large two-story home, filled with too many painful memories. By 1948, Ralph and Eva had downsized to a smaller residence at 1005 Warren Street.[392]

Now retired, Ralph kept busy painting houses to earn additional money. Eva, meanwhile, immersed herself in her church and civic interests. Eva continued her observance of the doctrine outlined by the Church of Christ, Scientist, and was a regular attendee and verbal participant at the group's new edifice, at 301 West Grand Avenue. While at church, the normally meek and reserved Eva frequently orated sermon readings and gave oral introductions for visiting lecturers. By all appearances, Eva's faith in God remained strong after her son's untimely death.[393]

Eva also served as an officer in the Chippewa Chapter of the Gold Star Mothers. At least twenty-eight Chippewa Falls matriarchs lost a son during World War II, while another four lost a son during the Korean conflict. Eva was a regular attendee at the meetings, which were held in the downtown American Legion Hall named after her son. Over the years, she was a hostess at the hall and officially served as chaplain or assistant conductress for the group. Together, these heroic women enjoyed each other's fellowship, shared meals together and organized fundraisers, such as bazaars or card-playing tournaments. The money raised would often be given to the Veterans Hospital in Tomah or, sometimes, to those suffering locally from polio. It was here that Eva found additional emotional strength, as each woman present was bound by similar pain and a common sacrifice.[394]

Above all else, Ralph and Eva looked forward to spending time with their eldest son, Robert; their daughter-in-law, Marie; and their six grandchildren, Carl, Gerald, David, Earl, Evelyne and now Barbara, born in 1951. Any earlier disappointment the parents felt toward Robert seemed to have dissipated long ago. Robert had carved out for himself a wonderful family and a solid career as a respected mechanic and earned the respect of both of his parents.

On Sunday, April 3, 1960, Robert and Marie Kramer hosted a "Golden Wedding Anniversary" event for Ralph and Eva. Eva wore a "grey dress with a corsage of yellow carnations," while Ralph was attired in a "dark blue suit, accented with a yellow carnation boutonniere." They received many "lovely gifts and money," including a "beautiful bouquet of yellow roses from the First Church of Christ, Scientist," and a "lovely gold swan filled with yellow jonquils" from the Gold Star Mothers. After a brief history of their marriage was read aloud, several of the grandchildren offered tributes of their own. Carl, now age twenty-six, arranged the program and concluded the event with a prayer; Earl, nineteen, sang two solos; Evelyne, eighteen, cut the cake and played piano; and Barbara, nine, presided over

Possibly the last photograph taken of Ralph and Eva Kramer together, shown here with Robert and Marie's dog Lady, mid-1960s. *Author's collection.*

the guestbook.[395] Ralph and Eva's grandsons Gerald, twenty-three,[396]and David twenty-one,[397] were not present, as both were away serving in the United States Army.

With each passing year, as Ralph and Eva lived to proudly see their grandchildren grow into successful adults, they were left to wonder how Harry's life would have turned out. Would he have moved out to one of the western states or returned home to Chippewa Falls? What occupation would he have chosen for himself? What special young woman would their son have courted? How many children would they have had? In a revealing letter that he wrote to the leaders of the Northern Pacific Railroad, Ralph talked about his son and how the railroad had played a role in aiding his development. He wrote, "I think it was in 1938 I wrote your office for timetables and information relative to a trip to Yellowstone Park that I was giving my son as a graduation president. He spent a month out there and had a wonderful time....We did not know then," Ralph added, "that he would so soon reach a man's stature and give his country the last full measure of devotion on board his battleship." The father concluded, "I know his ringing, spontaneous laughter still echoes in the canyons of Yellowstone, for he enjoyed life to the full."[398]

Ralph Kramer visiting the home of his eldest son, Robert, circa 1961. Robert and Marie's dog Lady is also shown. *Author's collection.*

By 1966, Ralph's health had noticeably deteriorated. At age eighty-two, several decades of chain-smoking cigarettes had taken its toll. Adding to his physical decline was the mental anguish associated with the upcoming twenty-fifth anniversary of the attack on Pearl Harbor. For better or for worse, Ralph and Eva had reasonably managed their sorrow by compartmentalizing their son into a semi-distant memory. Twenty-five years later, the heartache still taxed their souls. On December 2, 1966, just five days prior to the infamous milestone, Ralph Kramer succumbed to death at St. Joseph's Hospital in Chippewa Falls. His funeral was held at Hogseth-Pederson Funeral Chapel, as Mabel Cook of the Church of Christ, Scientist, officiated.[399]

With her husband of fifty-six years having passed, Eva was left both heartbroken and financially vulnerable. For the vast majority of her life, Ralph had been her rock, a strong and reliable force in the household. That Christmas season, Eva would have to endure the somber anniversary of Harry's death alone.

By April of the following year, Robert moved his mother in with him, Marie and their remaining children. With the 1005 Warren Street house officially available on the market, a "thrift sale" was advertised as having a "davenport and chair, refrigerator, kitchen cabinet, tables, chairs, dishes, fruit jars, and miscellaneous" items for sale.[400] On May 23, a photo advertisement in the *Chippewa Herald-Telegram* showed Ralph and Eva's old house with the caption: "SOLD! SOLD! SOLD! Home at 1005 Warren Street. Best wishes to the new owners for many years of happy living in their new home! — Bob Kleinheinz, Realtor"[401] All Eva had left was her clothing and personal effects, some items important to Ralph and a box of Harry's mementos. Despite her grief and loneliness, she had her dutiful son, Robert, Marie and their children to help look after her at the end.

On April 6, 1968, on the exact one-year anniversary of the thrift sale and two days following the assassination of Martin Luther King Jr., Eva Kramer died at the age of eighty-eight. In a funeral similar to her husband's, Mabel Cook officiated a Church of Christ, Scientist service at the Hogseth-Pederson Funeral Chapel. Eva's body was interred next to Ralph, the love of her life, in Forest Hill Cemetery in Chippewa Falls.[402]

Robert Kramer, fifty-seven, remained as the final living vestige of the Kramer household. The hardworking Robert continued his employment as an auto mechanic until his retirement from Henry Anderson Motors in Chippewa Falls in 1974. Despite recurring back problems and blindness in one eye, Robert was not the type of man who was easily slowed. His strong work ethic kept him busy around the house, as he loved working on projects that required his hands and a good set of tools. Together, Robert and Marie took pride in the successes of their six children, as well as the arrival of thirteen grandchildren.[403]

On March 13, 1986, Robert faced what was arguably the most devastating personal loss since the death of his brother. Marie, his wife of fifty-two years, passed away from heart disease at St. Joseph's Hospital in Chippewa Falls. The family had her buried in the city's Forest Hill Cemetery, opposite Marie's parents, as the trio shared a common headstone. On the back side of the marker were the engraved names of Anton and Elsie Grip, Marie's parents, who died in 1962 and 1985, respectively. The front side of the stone was reserved for Robert and Marie.[404] For the first time in his life, Robert was generationally alone.

As Robert grappled with the reality of life without Marie, he was left to forge a new version of life for himself. He began to take side trips around the area, built himself an artful workbench he had always wanted and continued to tinker around the house. Now free from the watchful critique of his in-laws, Robert even expanded the size of his home. He had always wanted to give his family more room with an addition, but Anton and Elsie had made it known it wasn't necessary. Now, it was just Robert's decision. Relatives recall how he found a lot of pride and happiness in that expansion project, as if it was symbolic of something deeper and more meaningful. Finally, he had taken his own stand for himself: a renovated home for a remodeled man.[405]

This was also when Robert began to talk openly about his brother to Annie, his teenage granddaughter. With the exception of Marie, Robert had never felt comfortable talking about Harry with anyone. But in Annie's presence, "Grandpa Bob" let his guard down. He told her how close he and Harry had been, despite their eight-year age difference. He revealed how the two boys had grown up sharing the same bedroom and together maintained a memory box filled with trinkets each boy would add. Because of this closeness, the two shared secrets and told stories to one another. When school got canceled due to snow, Robert and Harry went sledding together, with the assistance of Eva's homemade hot chocolate. As "Grandpa Bob" shared these memories, Annie picked up on a deep sadness, as well. Robert would get teary-eyed and explain how sweet a kid Harry was and how he was just starting to come into his own in the world. He revealed to her how Harry had been the godfather of Annie's father, David, and how "ever present" the young Harry was for his nieces and nephews.[406] When talking to Annie, it seemed Robert was able to honor his brother without competing against his larger-than-life shadow. He had never been jealous of Harry, only proud. Yet he spent nearly a lifetime feeling marginalized by others because of comparisons other people made. Robert, it seemed, was finding his own inner peace.

During the remaining years of his life, Robert remained in his home in Anson Township. He stayed industrious, well-read and connected to his children, grandchildren and great-grandchildren. Partnered with a package of orange slice candies, the aging patriarch liked to watch episodes of the *Lawrence Welk Show*, *Hee Haw* and reruns of *I Dream of Jeannie*, where he maintained a bit of a celebrity crush on its leading actress, Barbara Eden. Nine years after Marie's death, on August 11, 1995, the eighty-four-year-old

Robert died in his home, from congestive heart failure. At his funeral, his granddaughter Annie, now in her early twenties, sang "Amazing Grace," just prior to his interment beside his beloved Marie.[407] Robert had finally been reunited with Marie, Ralph and Eva and his brother, Harry.

Robert's passing marked the end of an era and the passing of a generational torch in the Kramer family. The couple's six children naturally became the caretakers of their family's personal history, including that of their uncle Harry. Unfortunately, most of the memories, stories, anecdotes and details associated with Harry are now lost to time. Much of what has remained was pieced together through personal vignettes recounted by each of his descendants. Harry's oldest nephew, Carl, was just seven years old when Pearl Harbor happened. He fondly recalled Harry playing games with him and his brother Gerald, as well as Harry assisting in the installation of a backyard basketball hoop. Carl also remembered overhearing a conversation in which his Grandpa Ralph vented his anger over Harry's death to Robert. "It shouldn't have happened!" Ralph exclaimed, as he never forgave navy officials for ignoring the warning signs.

Carl and Gerald's younger brothers, David and Earl, who were ages three and one when Harry died, were too young to recall him, while their sisters, Evelyne and Barbara, didn't arrive until after his death. Over the subsequent years, Evelyne recalled how her mother, Marie, would cry when she would see Pearl Harbor–related items on television. On one occasion, when Evelyne asked her mother why she was upset, Marie responded, "You'll understand when you get older what it feels like to lose someone close to you."

Out of all the children, it was Barbara, born in 1951, who was most surprised to learn about Harry. Born ten years after her uncle's death, she first learned of him when a teacher from Chippewa Falls High School approached her with the gift of a wooden plaque in the shape of a shield. The teacher said that the plaque had been hanging on a wall in the school for many years and that school officials thought it was best to give it to someone in the family. The twenty-five-year-old memorial, now outdated-looking and partially faded, read:

In Memory of
Harry Kramer
Born Nov. 10, 1919
Killed at Pearl Harbor—December 7, 1941
Class of 1938[408]

As a high school student in the late 1960s, Barbara didn't know what to make of it. She had never heard of this man. Were they related? She took the plaque home to her mother. Without providing much context, Marie informed her youngest daughter that Harry was her father's only brother and that he had died at Pearl Harbor. The wooden plaque, which had begun its journey at the Harry W. Kramer Memorial Program on March 31, 1942, was placed in a cardboard box of other Harry Kramer artifacts and safely stored away. For reasons unknown, either through oversight or intent, no suitable replacement was erected in the school. Harry's memory, it seemed, was disappearing from the public's consciousness.

Now, over eight decades after his death, Harry Wellington Kramer's memory has begun to resurface in his beloved Chippewa Falls. The Flags 4 the Fallen club is dedicated to the identification and honoring of our school's fallen soldiers. In 2017, I had the privilege of leading one group of students and staff to Pearl Harbor. One of the student travelers was Michael Kramer, who is the great-great-nephew of Harry. Michael's father, Jim Kramer, was the son of Carl Kramer, the eldest boy of Robert and Marie.

Michael Kramer's pilgrimage to Harry's grave, in 2017, was only the second time that a blood relative had visited the site, as his second cousin Annie Kramer visited first in 2007. Prior to our departure to Honolulu, I gave the sixteen-year-old sophomore printed copies of Harry's letters. During the long flight, while both of us painstakingly read through each of the letters, I couldn't help but take a long glance at Michael. It dawned on me then just how similar the two men were in persona. Like Harry, Michael was an old soul who was known for his maturity, decency and kindheartedness. He was also quiet, generous and extremely well respected. After our arrival in Hawaii, Michael and I broke away from the rest of the group during free time and sought out the various locations Harry visited while he had been there. As best we could, we attempted to recreate the photos where his great-great-uncle Harry had stood, including those taken on famed Waikiki Beach. Each turned out to be both eerie, yet magical.

But it was the visit to Harry's gravesite, at the National Memorial Cemetery of the Pacific, or the Punchbowl, that was so moving and memorable for all the staff and student travelers. From a distance, everyone watched as Michael knelt down at Harry's grave to pay his respects. For nearly forty minutes, Michael quietly and privately conveyed the family's condolences, sent by dozens of relatives spanning several generations of Robert and Marie's children, grandchildren, great-grandchildren and now great-great-grandchildren.

Left: Original wooden memorial plaque first unveiled at Chippewa Falls Senior High School in 1942. It was returned to the family in the late 1960s. *Author's collection.*

Below: Michael Kramer reading his great-great-uncle's letters on the airplane ride to Hawaii, 2017. *Author's collection.*

Above: Great-great-nephew Michael Kramer recreating Harry's beach photo, 2017. *Author's collection.*

Left: Author John E. Kinville recreating Harry's hotel photo, 2017. *Author's collection.*

Opposite, top: Michael Kramer making a pilgrimage on behalf of the entire extended Kramer family, 2017. *Author's collection.*

Opposite, bottom: Harry's headstone, Plot F Grave 675, 2017. *Author's collection.*

Left: Author John E. Kinville and Michael Kramer at Harry's grave, 2017. *Author's collection.*

Opposite: Today, at Chippewa Falls Senior High School, a much more extensive tribute, including Harry's photos and war medals and a replica of his navy uniform, has returned to the halls of Chippewa Falls Senior High School. The original wooden memorial plaque, first unveiled to Ralph and Eva Kramer in 1943, is also part of the display, 2022. *Author's collection.*

In the years I have been researching him, Harry has become near and dear to my own heart. In many ways, he feels like the brother I never had. That is why I celebrated this book's completion by getting a forearm tattoo featuring Harry's signature from his Oath of Allegiance certificate. With him becoming such an indelible part of my life, I, too—like Ralph, Eva, Robert and Marie—am left pondering unanswered questions that I may never get sufficient answers to. First, what were the specific circumstances of Harry's death? Had Pearl Harbor not been such a large-scale tragedy, the U.S. Navy would have kept more detailed records pertaining to individual sailors' deaths. Secondly, why was his body not identified until 1949? Harry was immediately listed on the *California*'s initial list of 37 known deceased, while an additional 117 still were labeled as missing. Whether that distinction was based on a body presumed to be his or a fellow sailor's eyewitness account may never be known. Thirdly, was the corpse labeled "Unknown X-104" correctly identified? While a modern-day exhumation

and DNA test would likely provide a definitive answer, twenty-five burials associated with *California* have yet to be positively identified.[409] It's possible some bodies may have been incorrectly identified back in 1949. Lastly, and most importantly, what would Harry have achieved had he been blessed with a longer life?

Today, located in the student commons area of Chippewa Falls Senior High School, you will find a large memorial display case dedicated to Harry Wellington Kramer. It contains an assortment of his photos, his casket flag, his war medals and a replica of his navy uniform. The wooden shield-shaped memorial plaque is back as part of the display. Together, between the school's updated memorial display and the release of this book, we can keep Harry's memory, service and sacrifice in the forefront of public consciousness, so future generations can learn his story. Hopefully, these tributes can also serve as an inspiration for others to rediscover their own community's heroes, as there are countless numbers of military patriots whose contributions have been lost. In the meantime, if you ever travel to Honolulu and visit the Punchbowl, please bid Harry a grateful "aloha" and let him know that he is not forgotten.

APPENDIX

CLASS OF SERVICE

This is a full-rate Telegram or Cablegram unless its deferred character is indicated by a suitable symbol above or preceding the address.

WESTERN UNION

1220

SYMBOLS

DL = Day Letter
NT = Overnight Telegram
LC = Deferred Cable
NLT = Cable Night Letter
Ship Radiogram

R. B. WHITE
PRESIDENT

NEWCOMB CARLTON
CHAIRMAN OF THE BOARD

J. C. WILLEVER
FIRST VICE-PRESIDENT

The filing time shown in the date line on telegrams and day letters is STANDARD TIME at point of origin. Time of receipt is STANDARD TIME at point of destination

```
16M MN  99 GOVT  9  EXTRA  DUP OF  TELE SENT TO KY RR OFFICE CFM

WASHINGTON D C  246A  DEC  16 1941

RALPH B KRAMER

        21  WELLS  ST  CHIPPEWAFALLS WIS
THE NAVY DEPARTMENT DEEPLY REGRETS TO INFORM YOU THAT YOUR SON
HARRY  WELLINGTON KRAMER  FIREMAN FIRST CLASS U S NAVY  WAS LOST
IN ACTION IN THE  PERFORMANCE OF HIS DUTY AND IN THE  SERVICE OF
HIS COUNTRY.  THE DEPARTMENT EXTENDS TO YOU ITS SINCEREST SYMPATHY
IN YOUR GREAT LOSS, TO PREVENT POSSIBLE AID TO OUR ENEMIES PLEASE
DO NOT  DIVULGE THE NAME OF HIS SHIP OR  STATION, IF REMAINS ARE
RECOVERED THEY WILL BE INTERRED  TEMPORARILY IN THE LOCALITY
WHERE DEATH OCCURRED AND YOU WILL BE NOTIFIED ACCORDINGLY
            REAR ADMIRAL C W NIMITZ  CHIEF OF THE BUREAU  OF
            NAVAGATION
                    900A  DEC 16
```

THE COMPANY WILL APPRECIATE SUGGESTIONS FROM ITS PATRONS CONCERNING ITS SERVICE

Original Western Union telegraph informing Ralph and Eva Kramer of their son's death, 1941. *Author's collection.*

Kramer, Harry Wellington
U.S.S. California

Enlistment ··· January 24, 1940 ··· Minneapolis, Minn.
Expires ··· January 23, 1946 "

Reported on board ··· March 26, 1940 — From ··· NTS, Great Lakes
Received in A division ··· August 6, 1940 — From ··· 2nd. Division

Rate ··· Fireman $\frac{3}{c}$ Date effective ··· August 5, 1940
" ··· Fireman $\frac{2}{c}$ " " ··· February 16, 1941
" Fireman $\frac{1}{c}$ " " ··· July 1, 1941

Home Address ··· 21 Wells Street, Chippewa Falls, Wisconsin
Ships Address ··· U.S.S. California, Long Beach, California - Box 37
Date of Birth ··· November 10, 1919
Serice Number ··· 328-65-18
Pay Number ··· 5-473 - 5-240 - 4-317
Billet Number ··· A-131
Bunk Number ··· A-83-B A-83-M

Harry's handwritten ship's log from the USS *California*, page 1, 1940–41. *Author's collection.*

L O G . . . .

H.W. Kramer - A Div.   U.S.S. California

1940

Jan.

24 Sworn in at Minneapolis Recruiting Station.

"   Left Minneapolis by train, for Naval Training Station.

25 Arrived at Great Lakes Training Station, Illinois.

Mar.

23 Left Training station for California.

26 Came on board U.S.S. California, anchored off Long Beach, California.

April

3   Underway for the Hawaiian islands.

11 Anchored at Lahaina Roads.

21 Underway for maneuvers.

24 Anchor at Lahaina Roads

25 Underway for island of Oahu.

26 Anchor in Pearl Harbor.

May

13 Underway for Long Beach, California.

20 Anchor at Long Beach

22 Underway for Bremerton navy yard, Washington.

26 Dock at Bremerton yards.

Aug.

26 Underway for Long Beach.

29 Arrive at Long Beach.

Sept.

2   Underway for Hawaii.

5   Anchor in Pearl Harbor for mail.

5   Underway for Lahaina for maneuvers.

Harry's handwritten ship's log from the USS *California*, page 2, 1940–41. *Author's collection.*

9	Leave Lahaina.
13	Anchor at Pearl Harbor.
23	Underway for gunnery drills.
24	Anchor at Lahaina.
30	Underway

Oct.

4	Anchor at Lahaina
7	Underway for maneuvers.
12	Anchor at Pearl Harbor.
28	Underway for maneuvers.

Nov.

1	Anchor off Waikiki.
4	Underway
6	Anchor off Waikiki.
8	Underway for Long Beach, California.
14	Anchor at Long Beach.

Dec.

2	Underway for Bremerton, Washington.
6	Dock at Bremerton yards.
26	Underway for Long Beach.
30	Anchor off Long Beach.

1941
Jan.

6	Underway for drills.
10	Anchor off Long Beach.
13	Underway for drills.
17	Anchor off Long Beach for liberty.
20	Underway for Bremerton, Washington.
24	Dock at Bremerton yards.

Harry's handwritten ship's log from the USS *California*, page 3, 1940–41. *Author's collection.*

```
1941
April
   9  Underway for San Francisco
  11  Anchor off Treasure Island in Frisco Bay
  12  Underway to Hawaiian Islands
  18  Dock at Pier in Pearl Harbor
  26  Underway for maneuvers
  30  Stop off Honolulu to put plane aboard the Swan
May
   5  Anchor in Pearl Harbor
  14  Underway For Maneuvers
  23  Anchor In Pearl Harbor
   ?  Underway For Maneuvers
   5  Anchor In Pearl Harbor
  14  Underway For Maneuvers
  23  Anchored At Pearl Harbor
June
   2  Underway For Maneuvers
   6  Anchored At Pearl Harbor
  25  Underway For Maneuvers
July  3  Anchored at Pearl Harbor
  "  16  Underway For Maneuvers
  23  Anchor at Pearl Harbor

Aug  6  Underway for maneuvers
  14  Anchor in Pearl Harbor
  27  Underway for maneuvers
```

Harry's handwritten ship's log from the USS *California*, page 4, 1940–41. *Author's collection.*

Author's forearm tattoo, featuring Harry's U.S. Navy Oath of Allegiance signature, 2022. *Author's collection.*

NOTES

Preface

1. "Remembering Pearl Harbor: A Pearl Harbor Fact Sheet," National WWII Museum, https://www.census.gov/history/pdf/pearl-harbor-fact-sheet-1.pdf.

Introduction

2. "Harry W. Kramer Memorial Held," *Chippewa Herald-Telegram* (hereafter CHT), March 31, 1942.
3. Ibid.
4. Ibid.
5. Ibid.
6. Ibid.
7. Ibid.
8. "Card of Thanks," CHT, April 4, 1942.
9. Julia Kagan, "The Greatest Generation: Definition and Characteristics," Investopedia, April 26, 2021, https://www.investopedia.com/terms/t/the_greatest_generation.asp#:~:text=The%20Greatest%20Generation%20is%20also,or%20the%20%22WWII%20Generation.%22.

Part I

10. Ada Buske, "Golden Wedding Day of Eva and Ralph Kramer," in *Personal Memories*, 1960. Personal collection of John E. Kinville.
11. "Kramer-Webb Wedding," *Eau Claire Leader-Telegram*, April 1, 1910.
12. Buske, "Golden Wedding Day."

13. "Kramer-Webb Wedding."
14. "To Have Headquarters Here," *Grand Forks Herald*, May 30, 1911.
15. Dinerman, "The Fedora Lounge Guide to Mackinaw Coats," The Fedora Louge, May 24, 2013, https://www.thefedoralounge.com/threads/the-fedora-lounge-guide-to-mackinaw-coats.72055/.
16. Marie Kramer, "Robert Kramer," in *Personal Memories*, 1980. Personal collection of John E. Kinville.
17. Evelyne Yungerberg Kramer and Earl Kramer (Harry Kramer's niece and nephew), interview by John E. Kinville, June 18–20, 2022.
18. Buske, "Golden Wedding Day."
19. Marie Kramer, "Robert Kramer."
20. Wikipedia, "Eau Claire Historical Population," accessed June 13, 2022.
21. "To Have Headquarters Here."
22. Marie Kramer, "Robert Kramer."
23. "Buys Residence Here," *Eau Claire Leader-Telegram*, January 26, 1919.
24. "Weather Archive—1919." Accessed June 16, 2022. http://wxarchive.uppermw.com/index.cfm?month=5&year=1919.
25. Register of Deeds, "Certificate of Live Birth—Harry Wellington Kramer," Eau Claire, Wisconsin, November 10, 1919.
26. Marie Kramer, "Robert Kramer."
27. Ibid.
28. "Harry Kramer Birthday," CHT, November 14, 1924.
29. Severa Sylvia Lemke, "Harry Kramer Report Cards," Chippewa County Public School report cards, 1926 and 1927. Personal collection of John E. Kinville.
30. "Wellington Webb of Anson Passes Away," CHT, November 30, 1923.
31. "Ralph Kramer," CHT, April 25, 1928.
32. Marie Kramer, "Robert Kramer."
33. Wikipedia, "Great Depression," accessed June 16, 2022. https://en.wikipedia.org/wiki/Great_Depression.
34. "Moving Here," CHT, October 28, 1930.
35. "Butler Co.," CHT, May 22, 1929.
36. "Phillips 66," CHT, July 16, 1930.
37. Marie Kramer, "Robert Kramer."
38. Ibid.
39. "Has Chippewa History," CHT, June 14, 1937.
40. Evelyne Yungerberg Kramer and Earl Kramer, interview.
41. Marie Kramer, "Robert Kramer."
42. Evelyne Yungerberg Kramer and Earl Kramer, interview.
43. "Anson Items," CHT, August 14, 1936.
44. Annie Kramer, phone interview by John E. Kinville, July 26, 2022.
45. "Chippewa High School News," CHT, May 16, 1936.
46. "Chippewa Falls High School News—Machine Shop," CHT, March 7, 1938.
47. "Christian Science Society," CHT, April 26, 1926.

48. Donna Bourget, Anne Keller and James Schuh, *Irvine Park and Smaller Chippewa Falls Parks: The Bear Facts* (Chippewa Falls, WI: Chippewa County Historical Society, 2018).

49. "Morris Anderson in the 1930 US Federal Census," Ancestry.com, accessed June 21, 2022, https://www.ancestry.com/discoveryui-content/view/59909529:6224.

50. Ibid.

51. Jean Selden (Jack Selden's sister), interview by John E. Kinville, December 23, 2021.

52. Chippewa Falls High School, *Monocle*, 1938.

53. "Hold Class Picnic," CHT, June 2, 1938.

54. "129 Students Get Diplomas," CHT, June 4, 1938.

55. Ibid.

56. "Just Returned," CHT, August 29, 1938.

57. "Enters Naval Service," CHT, January 22, 1940.

58. Harry Wellington Kramer, U.S. Navy NRB Form 10, January 24, 1940, personal collection of John E. Kinville.

59. Ibid.

60. "Join Navy," *Eau Claire Leader-Telegram*, January 27, 1940.

Part II

61. Naval History and Heritage Command, "Naval Station Great Lakes, Illinois," August 31, 2018, https://www.history.navy.mil/browse-by-topic/organization-and-administration/installations/naval-station-great-lakes.html.

62. Francis Buzzell, *The Great Lakes Naval Training Station: A History* (Wolcott, NY: Scholar's Choice, 2015).

63. Harry Wellington Kramer, letter no. 1, February 11, 1940, personal collection of John Kinville.

64. "Embargo Action Awaited as Japanese Trade Pact Ends," CHT, January 26, 1940.

65. "House Rejects Guam Proposal," CHT, February 16, 1940.

66. "Italy to Double Her Air Forces," CHT, February 3, 1940.

67. "Say Americans Killed by Nazis in Poland," CHT, February 8, 1940.

68. "Aides of FDR Go to Europe," CHT, February 17, 1940.

69. Harry Wellington Kramer, letter no. 2, February 18, 1940, personal collection of John Kinville.

70. "Welles in Conference with Italian Premier," CHT, February 26, 1940.

71. "Germany Is Set to Continue Her Present Setup," CHT, February 29, 1940.

72. "Planes and Troops Are Active on West Front," CHT, February 27, 1940.

73. "Air, Sea Warfare Renewed Between Britain and Nazis," CHT, March 1, 1940.

74. "FDR Inspects Panama Defense," CHT, February 26, 1940.

75. "Cracker Jack," *Evening World*, March 6, 1916.

76. Harry Wellington Kramer, letter no. 3, March 3, 1940, personal collection of John Kinville.

77. PBS, "Censorship!," 2021, accessed December 27, 2022, https://www.pbs. org/wgbh/americanexperience/features/warletters-censorship/.
78. "Italian Cargo Ships Are Seized by British Ships," CHT, March 5, 1940.
79. "Nazis Mark Time in Peace Efforts," CHT, March 11, 1940.
80. Ibid.
81. Harry Wellington Kramer, letter no. 4, March 14, 1940, personal collection of John Kinville.
82. "Report Berlin-Rome Axis to Be Extended to Moscow," CHT, March 18, 1940.
83. Ibid.
84. "Declares Japanese Navy Is Ready," CHT, March 23, 1940.
85. Harry Wellington Kramer, letter no. 5, March 25, 1940, personal collection of John Kinville.
86. Mary Baker Eddy, *Science and Health with Key to the Scriptures* (Boston, MA: W.F. Brown, 1872).
87. Harry Wellington Kramer, letter no. 6, March 25, 1940, personal collection of John Kinville.
88. "Nazis Claim President Planned Entering War," CHT, March 29, 1940.
89. "German 'War' Charges Denied at Washington," CHT, March 30, 1940.
90. "Churchill in Charge of British War Setup," CHT, April 4, 1940.
91. "New Government Setup in China," CHT, March 30, 1940.
92. George F. Gruner, *Blue Water Beat: The Two Lives of the Battleship USS* California (San Francisco, CA: Glencannon Press, 2015).
93. Mary Pukui and Samuel Elbert, *Place Names of Hawaii* (Honolulu: University of Hawaii Press, 1974).
94. United States Census Bureau, "Hawaii: Population of Counties by Minor Civil Divisions," 1940 United States Census.
95. Harry Wellington Kramer, letter no. 7, April 13, 1940, personal collection of John Kinville.
96. "Hitler Declares War on Between Norway, Germany," CHT, April 27, 1940.
97. "FDR Proclaims Nazi, Norway War," CHT, April 25, 1940.
98. "American Wish to Live in Peace, Says FDR," CHT, April 15, 1940.
99. Joshua Schick, "Routine in Paradise: The US Navy in Pearl Harbor," National World War II Museum, October 9, 2021, https://www.nationalww2museum. org/war/articles/us-navy-before-pearl-harbor-attack.
100. Ibid.
101. Harry Wellington Kramer, letter no. 8, May 5, 1940, personal collection of John Kinville.
102. Harry Wellington Kramer, letter no. 9, May 6, 1940, personal collection of John Kinville.
103. "Chamberlain Quits, Churchill Premier; Germans Invade Belgium and Holland," CHT, May 10, 1940.
104. Mount Holyoke College, "Winston Churchill: Speech to Parliament," May 13, 1940, accessed January 22, 2022, https://www.mtholyoke.edu/acad/intrel/ speech/blood.htm.

105. "Germans Say Maginot Line Pierced," CHT, May 15, 1940.
106. "FDR Asks Another Billion for Defense," CHT, May 31, 1940.
107. "Nazis Capture Paris: France on Edge of Complete Disaster," CHT, June 14, 1940.
108. Harry Wellington Kramer, letter no. 10, June 15, 1940, personal collection of John Kinville.
109. "Germany Clears Boards for Drive against England," CHT, June 24, 1940.
110. "Japanese Warn Western Powers," CHT, June 29, 1940.
111. "Republicans Name Willkie and McNary," CHT, June 28, 1940.
112. "Mildred Grant in the 1940 United States Federal Census," Ancestry.com, https://www.ancestry.com/discoveryui-content/view/64790987:2442.
113. Harry Wellington Kramer, letter no. 12, July 7, 1940, personal collection of John Kinville.
114. "Says FDR Not Candidate, but Is to Be Nominated," CHT, July 9, 1940.
115. "US to Purchase 629 New Tanks," CHT, July 9, 1940.
116. Harry Wellington Kramer, letter no. 13, July 12, 1940, personal collection of John Kinville.
117. "Three-Fold Attack on Britain Is Nazi Fascist Program," CHT, July 9, 1940.
118. "Wallace Due to be FDR Running Mate," CHT, July 18, 1940.
119. "Peace or Destruction, Hitler Warning," CHT, July 19, 1940.
120. "Britain to Buy 3,000 Planes a Month in US," CHT, July 25, 1940.
121. "Laverne Zenner Bride of William Howie," CHT, July 22, 1940.
122. Harry Wellington Kramer, letter no. 14, August 1, 1940, personal collection of John Kinville.
123. "Mildred Grant."
124. "Britain Now Fears Break with Japanese Is Near," CHT, August 1, 1940.
125. "Britain Says Hamburg in Ruins," CHT, August 2, 1940.
126. "Churchill Inspects a Tommy Gun," CHT, August 3, 1940.
127. "Pershing Urges Aid for British," CHT, August 5, 1940.
128. "Lindbergh Sees Danger of War," CHT, August 5, 1940.
129. "Japan Protests Embargo on Oil," CHT, August 3, 1940.
130. "Opening Day at Fair Draws Huge Crowd," CHT, August 6, 1940.
131. "Residents Throng Fairgrounds," CHT, August 7, 1940.
132. "Thrill Program to Feature Fair Friday," CHT, August 8, 1940.
133. Harry Wellington Kramer, letter no. 15, August 16, 1940, personal collection of John Kinville.
134. "Hitler Declares British Isles under Blockade," CHT, August 17, 1940.
135. "Willkie Says Roosevelt Courts War," CHT, August 17, 1940.
136. "President Asks Prompt Action on Draft Bill," CHT, August 23, 1940.
137. Harry Wellington Kramer, letter no. 16, September 2, 1940, personal collection of John Kinville.
138. "US Gains Bases in Trade for Destroyers," CHT, September 3, 1940.
139. "US Speeds Transfer of Destroyers to Britain," CHT, September 4, 1940.
140. "Churchill Warns Parliament US Is Not in War," CHT, September 5, 1940.

141. Editors of Encyclopaedia Britannica, "The Blitz," last updated August 31, 2022, https://www.britannica.com/event/the-Blitz.

142. Wayne S. Cole, *America First: The Battle against Intervention, 1940–1941* (Madison: University of Wisconsin Press, 1953).

143. Meilan Solly, "The True History behind 'The Plot against America,'" *Smithsonian Magazine*, March 16, 2020.

144. "Contracts for 201 US Warships Are Awarded by Navy," CHT, September 9, 1940.

145. "$125,000 US Contract Secured by Woolen Mill," CHT, September 14, 1940.

146. "US Draft Bill Is Passed by Both Houses of Congress," CHT, September 14, 1940.

147. "FDR Reaffirms Stand to Keep War from US," CHT, September 12, 1940.

148. "Nazi Air Chief Leads Attack against London," CHT, September 16, 1940.

149. "Hitler, Mussolini Offer Spain Prize for Help in War," CHT, September 20, 1940.

150. "Await US Action on Japanese in Indochina," CHT, September 24, 1940.

151. "Fascists Sign Anti-US Pact," CHT, September 27, 1940.

152. "Japanese Press Sees Clash with America," CHT, September 27, 1940.

153. "Jack Larson," CHT, December 6, 1941.

154. "Enlists in Navy," CHT, May 19, 1939.

155. U.S. Census, 1930, Ancestry.com, https://www.ancestry.com/discoveryui-content/view/59913504:6224.

156. "Runs Down Man; Gets Three Months," CHT, September 27, 1940.

157. "Mrs. Dayton Cook Taken by Death," CHT, April 6, 1945.

158. "Churchill Defies Japanese, to Open Burma Road," CHT, October 8, 1940.

159. "Pacific Fleet of US Is Now Being 'Groomed,'" CHT, October 9, 1940.

160. "Willkie Says FDR May Talk Nation into War," CHT, October 14, 1940.

161. The Royal Hawaiian Resort Waikīkī, "History Overview," accessed February 15, 2022, https://www.royal-hawaiian.com/history-overview/.

162. Harry Wellington Kramer, letter no. 18, October 27, 1940, personal collection of John Kinville.

163. "Drawing Covers Seventeen Hours and 31 Minutes," CHT, October 30, 1940.

164. "First Number Drawn Is 158," CHT, October 29, 1940.

165. "Mortimer Anderson—US World War II Army Records," 1940, Ancestry.com.

166. "Robert Kramer—US World War II Draft Card," 1940, Ancestry.com.

167. "Mortimer Anderson," Ancestry.com.

168. Wikipedia, "1940 United States Presidential Election," accessed February 17, 2022, https://en.wikipedia.org/wiki/1940_United_States_presidential_election.

169. "New Naval Ship Every 12 Days," CHT, December 6, 1940.

170. "Britain Will Get 12,000 More US Built Warplanes," CHT, November 8, 1940.

171. "Warsaw Jews in Walled Ghetto," CHT, November 15, 1940.
172. "Greco-Italian War Begins," CHT, October 28, 1940.
173. "Hitler Makes Bid for Russian Help in His New Order," CHT, November 12, 1940.
174. "State Shivers in Grip of Severe Cold Wave," CHT, December 3, 1940.
175. Harry Wellington Kramer, letter no. 19, December 18, 1940, personal collection of John Kinville.
176. "Four-Man Defense High Command Is Named by FDR," CHT, December 21, 1940.
177. "Woolen Mills Get US Order," CHT, December 20, 1940.
178. "Chippewa Glove Co. Awarded $94,000 Order," CHT, December 23, 1940.
179. "FDR Says Most People Ask Chance to Improve World," CHT, December 24, 1940.
180. Harry Wellington Kramer, letter no. 20, December 25, 1940, personal collection of John Kinville.
181. "Hitler Sends Warplanes to Mussolini's Assistance," CHT, January 2, 1941.
182. "Victory for FDR Lend-Lease Plan to Aid Britain Is Seen," CHT, January 4, 1941.
183. "Willkie Backs Lend-Lease Bill," CHT, January 17, 1941.
184. "Expect Defense Costs to Double Next Year," CHT, December 27, 1941.
185. "Progress Is Made in Defense Program," CHT, December 31, 1940.
186. "US Now to Have 3-Fleet Navy and Add 42,000 Men," CHT, January 8, 1941.
187. "President Asks Budget of 17½ Billion, a Peacetime Record," CHT, January 8, 1941.
188. "Knox Gives Strength of US and Axis Navies," CHT, January 17, 1941.
189. "Knox Sees Danger to US If Britain Loses," CHT, January 17, 1941.
190. "Japanese Stage Third Parley in Reaction to Stand of US," CHT, January 17, 1941.
191. WikiMili, "M. Eugene Durfee," last updated June 4, 2021, accessed May 22, 2022, https://wikimili.com/en/M._Eugene_Durfee.
192. Harry Wellington Kramer, letter no. 21, January 17, 1941, personal collection of John Kinville.
193. Los Angeles Almanac, "The Pike in Long Beach," accessed February 19, 2022, http://www.laalmanac.com/history/hi08ap.php.
194. National Weather Service, "Inauguration Weather," January 20, 1941, accessed February 19, 2022, https://www.weather.gov/lwx/events_Inauguration.
195. Yale Law School, "Third Inaugural Address of Franklin Roosevelt," January 20, 1941, accessed February 18, 2022, https://avalon.law.yale.edu/20th_century/froos3.asp.
196. "Wiley against Present Terms of Lend-Lease Bill," CHT, January 23, 1941.
197. "Lindbergh Says US and Britain Can't Win War," CHT, January 23, 1941.
198. "Bullitt Accuses Nazis, Urges Aid for Britain," CHT, January 25, 1941.

199. "Mussolini Aide Warns US of War Danger," CHT, January 29, 1941.
200. "Hitler in Threat to Sink Ships of United States," CHT, January 30, 1941.
201. "House Nears Vote on Lend-Lease Bill," CHT, February 8, 1941.
202. Harry Wellington Kramer, letter no. 22, February 10, 1941, personal collection of John Kinville.
203. "Willkie Asks Passage of Lend-Lease Bill," CHT, February 11, 1941.
204. "Wiley Asks Hull Report to Senate," CHT, February 14, 1941.
205. "Fear Japanese Set for New Grab in Far East," CHT, February 13, 1941.
206. "Benjamin A. Smith—US World War II Army Records," 1941, Ancestry.com.
207. "Mort Anderson—Joins Army Air Corps," CHT, February 18, 1941.
208. Harry Wellington Kramer, letter no. 23, February 14, 1941, personal collection of John Kinville.
209. "Franco and Mussolini Parley in Italy," CHT, February 12, 1941.
210. "Turkey and Bulgaria Sign New Non-Aggression Pact," CHT, February 17, 1941.
211. "Hitler Tries to Force Greeks to Make Peace," CHT, February 18, 1941.
212. "House Puts OK on Naval Bases," CHT, February 19, 1941.
213. Britannica, "Jitterbug," https://www.britannica.com/art/jitterbug.
214. "Musical Monday: You'll Find Out (1940)," Comet Over Hollywood (blog), October 29, 2018, https://cometoverhollywood.com/2018/10/29/musical-monday-youll-find-out-1940/.
215. Harry Wellington Kramer, letter no. 24, February 19, 1941, personal collection of John Kinville.
216. "OK Naval Public Works Program on Guam, Other Bases," CHT, March 20, 1941.
217. "FDR Will Seek Seven Billion Aid to Britain," CHT, March 11, 1941.
218. "Lend-Lease Bill Attacked by Wiley in Senate Speech," CHT, March 4, 1941.
219. "Plan 20,000 Planes for Great Britain in Next 18 Months," CHT, March 22, 1941.
220. "President Warns Americans of Acute War Situation," CHT, April 18, 1941.
221. "Bargain Basement—Williams Brothers," (business advertisement); "San Francisco Examiner," CHT, May 22, 1941.
222. MeasuringWorth.com, 1941, accessed 2022.
223. Walter Davenport, "Impregnable Pearl Harbor," Collier's, June 14, 1941.
224. Harry Wellington Kramer, letter no. 25, April 20, 1941, personal collection of John Kinville.
225. "Now Over Hump in Defense Efforts Says General Marshall," CHT, April 22, 1941.
226. "FDR Stresses Need of Greater Speed in Defense Production," CHT, May 2, 1941.
227. "Chippewa Shoe Leases Space to Increase Output," CHT, April 26, 1941.
228. "President Calls for More Big Bombers," CHT, May 6, 1941.
229. "Drastic Federal Income Tax Plan Meets Opposition," CHT, April 23, 1941.
230. ibiblio, "Gallup Poll Results," April 10–15, 1941, accessed 2022, http://ibiblio.org/pha/Gallup/Gallup%201941.htm.

231. "Col. Lindbergh Resigns Air Corps Reserve Post," CHT, April 28, 1941.
232. "Asks If Lindbergh Had Returned His Hitler Decoration," CHT, April 29, 1941.
233. ibiblio, "Gallup Poll Results," April 10–15, 1941, accessed 2022, http://ibiblio.org/pha/Gallup/Gallup%201941.htm.
234. "The Axis 1941: Hitler Breaks Even with Napoleon on Conquests," CHT, April 24, 1941.
235. "Attack on Northern Ireland Capital," CHT, May 5, 1941.
236. "Pilots Launch Biggest War Smash," CHT, May 9, 1941.
237. "Berlin Still Insists No. 3 Nazi Is Deranged," CHT, May 13, 1941.
238. Harry Wellington Kramer, letter no. 26, May 13, 1941, personal collection of John Kinville.
239. "Mediterranean Is Now Axis Sea," CHT, June 2, 1941.
240. "Battle for Suez Held Next Phase in Middle East," CHT, May 31, 1941.
241. "US Breaks with Vichy," CHT, May 16, 1941.
242. "Vichy Government Puts Ban on Jews," CHT, June 13, 1941.
243. "Will Defend America against Attack or Threat of Attack Warns President," CHT, May 28, 1941.
244. "US to Build Air Fleet of 40,000 Planes," CHT, June 5, 1941.
245. "Army Seizes Airplane Plant," CHT, July 9, 1941.
246. "US at War in Fact Says Il Duce," CHT, June 10, 1941.
247. "US Takes Grave View of Ship Sinking," CHT, June 10, 1941.
248. "President Freezes All Nazi and Fascist Assets," CHT, June 14, 1941.
249. "US Edict Bans All German Consulates," CHT, June 16, 1941.
250. Kramer, letter no. 27.
251. "Ralph D Kramer in the 1940 United States Federal Census," Ancestry.com, https://www.ancestry.com/discoveryui-content/view/78643809:2442.
252. Naval History and Heritage Command, "Airships & Dirigibles," July 22, 2021, https://www.history.navy.mil/browse-by-topic/exploration-and-innovation/airships-dirigibles.html.
253. Harry Wellington Kramer, letter no. 27, June 17, 1941, personal collection of John Kinville.
254. F. Barrows Colton, "Life in Our Fighting Fleet," National Geographic Magazine, June 1941, 671–702.
255. "President Calls Germany an Outlaw," CHT, June 20, 1941.
256. "Germans Reach Riga on Baltic Front," CHT, July 1, 1941.
257. "Franklin Roosevelt OK's Soviet Port: Permits US Vessels to Carry Arms to Russians," CHT, June 25, 1941.
258. "Stalin Urges Scorched Earth Policy," CHT, July 3, 1941.
259. "President Asks United Defense of This Country," CHT, July 5, 1941.
260. "US Occupies Iceland," CHT, July 7, 1941.
261. "Japan May Cut Off US Route to Russia," CHT, July 5, 1941.
262. Justin T. Broderick, "U.S. Navy: World War II Enlisted Rates: Engine Room Force, Artificer Branch," 2013, https://uniform-reference.net/insignia/usn/usn_ww2_enl_engine_room.html.

263. John R.K. Clark, "Nanakuli Beach," Hawai'i Beach Safety, accessed April 3, 2022. https://hawaiibeachsafety.com/oahu/nanakuli-beach.
264. Harry Wellington Kramer, letter no. 28, July 12, 1941, personal collection of John Kinville.
265. Don J. Hibbard, "First Church of Christ, Scientist," Society of Architectural Historians, accessed April 4, 2022, https://sah-archipedia.org/buildings/HI-01-OA112.
266. Don Hibbard, Glenn Mason and Karen Weitze, *Hart Wood: Architectural Regionalism in Hawaii* (Honolulu: University of Hawaii Press, 2010).
267. Kramer, letter no. 28.
268. "Gate to Moscow Open," CHT, July 19, 1941.
269. "Japanese Ready to Strike?" CHT, July 14, 1941.
270. "Japan Mobilizes Million More Men," CHT, July 25, 1941.
271. "America Will Retaliate against Japan," CHT, July 25, 1941.
272. "Heads Philippine Army," CHT, July 28, 1941.
273. "US Warships in Australia," CHT, August 5, 1941.
274. "Plan for USO Drive in County," CHT, July 16, 1941.
275. "Drive Nets 6,635 Pounds," CHT, July 30, 1941.
276. Ann Yoklavich, *Historic American Buildings Survey: US Naval Base, Pearl Harbor, Recreational Facilities* (Honolulu, HI: Mason Architects, 2004).
277. Harry Wellington Kramer, letter no. 29, August 5, 1941, personal collection of John Kinville.
278. Peter T. Young, "Camp Andrews," Images of Old Hawai'i, August 23, 2016, https://imagesofoldhawaii.com/camp-andrews/.
279. Kramer, letter no. 29.
280. Britannica, "Arthur Wellesley, 1st Duke of Wellington," https://www.britannica.com/biography/Arthur-Wellesley-1st-Duke-of-Wellington.
281. "1941," Billboard Top 100, accessed April 16, 2022, http://billboardtop100of.com/1941-2/.
282. IMDb, "Olivia de Havilland Awards," accessed April 16, 2022, https://www.imdb.com/name/nm0000014/awards.
283. "Nazis Say Drive on Leningrad Is Within 32 Miles," CHT, August 28, 1941.
284. "Britain Warns Japanese: Ready to Defend Thailand," CHT, August 6, 1941.
285. Office of the Historian (United States State Department), "The Atlantic Conference & Charter, 1941," accessed April 25, 2022, https://history.state.gov/milestones/1937-1945/atlantic-conf.
286. Ibid.
287. "Roosevelt and Churchill in Meeting at Sea Define Join War, Peace Aims: Two Leaders Pledge to Destroy Nazi Tyranny," CHT, August 14, 1941.
288. "Come and Get Us Say Nazis," CHT, August 15, 1941.
289. "Program to Include Agreement against Japan and to Aid Russia," CHT, August 14, 1941.
290. "Scoffs Churchill Threat but Fears What US May Do," CHT, August 26, 1941.

291. "President Selects Board of Seven to Speed Arms Output," CHT, August 29, 1941.
292. "8-Hour Day Law Suspended by Franklin Roosevelt," CHT, August 13, 1941.
293. "Franklin Roosevelt Signs Record Tax Measure," CHT, September 20, 1941.
294. "US Destroyer Attacked More Than Once by Submarine Asserts President," CHT, September 5, 1941.
295. "Expect Roosevelt to Demand Full Freedom of Seas," CHT, September 10, 1941.
296. "LaFollette Sees War Major Issue Next Fall," CHT, September 20, 1941.
297. "Lindbergh Fears Dictatorship Is Near in America," CHT, October 4, 1941.
298. "Chippewa Falls Retail Stores Join Nation Selling Defense Stamps/Bonds," CHT, September 17, 1941.
299. "Chippewa Men Seek Unit of Wisconsin Air Squadron Here," CHT, September 27, 1941.
300. Harry Wellington Kramer, letter no. 30, October 5, 1941, personal collection of John Kinville.
301. Ibid.
302. Ibid.
303. "Nazis Seek Knockout," CHT, October 7, 1941.
304. "US Destroyer Torpedoed off Iceland," CHT, October 17, 1941.
305. "House Votes 259 to 138 to Arm Ships," CHT, October 17, 1941.
306. "To Triple Air Corps," CHT, October 23, 1941.
307. "President Urges Full Speed Ahead to Smash Hitler," CHT, October 28, 1941.
308. "Wiley Opposed to Neutrality Shift," CHT, October 30, 1941.
309. "Report: Senators Will Scrap Ban on Combat Zones," CHT, October 24, 1941.
310. "Japanese Premier Calls for 'Iron Unity' to Fight against Encirclement," CHT, October 20, 1941.
311. "Japan Deathly Afraid of US Pacific Fleet," CHT, September 3, 1941.
312. Harry Wellington Kramer, letter no. 31, October 30, 1941, personal collection of John Kinville.
313. Ibid.
314. Ibid.
315. Ibid.
316. Ibid.
317. "US Destroyer Is Sunk," CHT, October 31, 1941.
318. "Beaverbrook Paper Says James Sinking Declaration of War," CHT, November 1, 1941.
319. "Billions of Lend-Lease Credit Granted Russia," CHT, November 7, 1941.
320. "Senate Votes to Revise Neutrality Act," CHT, November 8, 1941.
321. "American Merchant Vessels Regain Complete Freedom of Seas," CHT, November 14, 1941.
322. Harry Wellington Kramer, letter no. 32, November 17, 1941, personal collection of John Kinville.

323. Wikipedia, "List of English words of Hawaiian Origin," https://en.wikipedia.org/wiki/List_of_English_words_of_Hawaiian_origin.
324. Kramer, letter no. 32.
325. Ibid.
326. Harry Wellington Kramer, letter no. 33, November 17, 1941, personal collection of John Kinville.

Part III

327. "President Meets Two Japanese Envoys," CHT, November 27, 1941.
328. "Uneasy Peace Strains Pacific Tension While US Waits Japanese Moves," CHT, December 6, 1941.
329. "President Meets Congress Chiefs on Japan Crisis," CHT, December 4, 1941.
330. "Uneasy Peace."
331. Rachel Duensing, "How the Weather Impacted the Attack on Pearl Harbor," December 7, 2021, https://www.cbs17.com/news/national-news/how-the-weather-impacted-the-attack-on-pearl-harbor-80-years-ago/.
332. Pearl Harbor Tours, "Ships in Pearl Harbor, Wreckage and Memorials, Sharks and Hawaiian Names," accessed June 28, 2022, https://www.pearlharbortours.com/blog/things-you-dont-know/.
333. WallBuilders, "Pearl Harbor—Orders of the Day for the USS California," December 7, 2017, https://wallbuilders.com/pearl-harbor-orders-day-uss-california/.
334. United States Navy, *U.S.S.* California *Torpedo and Bomb Damage, December 7, 1941 Pearl Harbor*, November 28, 1942, http://www.researcheratlarge.com/Ships/BB44/PearlHarborDamageReport/.
335. United States Navy, "Material Condition Matters," February 1, 2018, https://www.navy.mil/Press-Office/News-Stories/Article/2250320/material-condition-matters/.
336. "Pearl Harbor Fact Sheet," National WWII Museum, accessed June 30, 2022, https://orbit.texthelp.com/?file=https://www.census.gov/history/pdf/pearl-harbor-fact-sheet-1.pdf.
337. Wikipedia, "United States Declaration of War on Japan," https://en.wikipedia.org/wiki/United_States_declaration_of_war_on_Japan.
338. George Gruner, "USS California: Losing the Prune Barge at Pearl Harbor," *Sea Classics*, July 1997.
339. United States Navy, U.S.S. California, 2.
340. Ibid.
341. Ibid, 3.
342. Ibid.
343. Ibid.
344. J.W. Bunkley, Log Book of the USS California, United States Navy and the National Archives, December 17, 1941.
345. "US Declares War on Japan," CHT, December 8, 1941.

346. Ibid.
347. Rear Admiral C.W. Nimitz, Western Union telegram to Ralph Kramer, December 16, 1941, personal collection of John E. Kinville.
348. Evelyne Yungerberg Kramer and Earl Kramer, interview.
349. Ibid.
350. "Chippewa Youth Killed in Action," *Eau Claire Leader-Telegram*, December 17, 1941.
351. "Chippewa Men in Hawaii Attacks," CHT, December 8, 1941.
352. "Wisconsin Deaths at Pearl Harbor," *Milwaukee Journal Sentinel*, December 6, 2016.
353. "Pearl Harbor Poem," CHT, December 20, 1941.
354. Mortimer Anderson, letter to Ralph Kramer, December 23, 1941, personal collection of John E. Kinville, 1941.
355. J.W. Bunkley, letter to Ralph Kramer, January 6, 1942, personal collection of John E. Kinville.
356. Frank Knox, letter to Ralph Kramer, January 14, 1942, personal collection of John E. Kinville.
357. Evelyne Yungerberg Kramer and Earl Kramer, interview.
358. Bunkley, letter to Ralph Kramer.
359. Nimitz, telegram to Kramer.
360. "Pearl Harbor Victim's Books Will Go to Pals," *Milwaukee Journal Sentinel*, February 15, 1942.
361. "Kramer Artifacts: Flag and Chevrons," July 1942, personal collection of John E. Kinville.
362. "Kramer Artifacts: Gold Star Citation and Flag," March 1943, personal collection of John E. Kinville.
363. "Kramer Artifacts: Purple Heart Citation and Medal," December 1943, personal collection of John E. Kinville.
364. "Research Starters: Worldwide Deaths in WWII," National World War II Museum, https://www.nationalww2museum.org/students-teachers/student-resources/research-starters/research-starters-worldwide-deaths-world-war.
365. "The Holocaust," National World War II Museum, https://www.nationalww2museum.org/war/articles/holocaust.
366. Seren Morris, "How Many People Died in Hiroshima and Nagasaki?" *Newsweek*, August 3, 2020, https://www.newsweek.com/how-many-people-died-hiroshima-nagasaki-japan-second-world-war-1522276.
367. Defense POW/MIA Accounting Agency, "USS California—World War II Fact Sheet," November 16, 2016.
368. C.A. Swanson, letter to Ralph Kramer, January 11, 1949, personal collection of John E. Kinville.
369. James B. Clearwater, letter to Ralph Kramer, November 1952, personal collection of John E. Kinville.

Afterword

370. John E. Kinville, "Flags 4 the Fallen List—Chippewa Falls High School 2020."
371. "PFC Robert E. Baldeshwiler," Find a Grave, 2020, https://www.findagrave.com/memorial/83071066/robert-e-baldeshwiler.
372. "Memorial Services Slated Sunday for PFC Desmond Kurth," CHT, May 4, 1945.
373. Peter Suciu, "Battleship USS California: How She Got Revenge for Pearl Harbor," *National Interest*, May 17, 2021, https://nationalinterest.org/blog/buzz/battleship-uss-california-how-she-got-revenge-pearl-harbor-185446.
374. Defense POW/MIA Accounting Agency, "USS California."
375. "Frank Nicoles Jr. Interment," *Eau Claire Leader-Telegram*, January 25, 2022, https://www.leadertelegram.com/frank-nicoles-jr-interment/image_fb06937d-e077-503e-a88f-54474ccf5aa4.html.
376. "USS Oklahoma Sailor Accounted for from World War II (Nicoles, F.)," Defense POW/MIA Accounting Agency, August 27, 2020, https://www.dpaa.mil/News-Stories/News-Releases/Article/1715137/uss-oklahoma-sailor-accounted-for-from-world-war-ii-nicoles-f/.
377. "1Lt. Lieutenant Thomas Lawrence Wood," Find a Grave, 2020, https://www.findagrave.com/memorial/56349899/thomas-lawrence-wood.
378. "Morien Eugene Durfee," *West Los Angeles Independent*, January 5, 1942.
379. "Ruth E. Liddiard," Find a Grave, 2020, https://www.findagrave.com/memorial/186669404/ruth-e-liddiard.
380. Wikipedia, "Navy Electronics Laboratory."
381. Carol Buteau Liddiard, interview by John E. Kinville, July 14, 2022.
382. "Dr. Hope H. Corey," *San Francisco Examiner*, August 14, 1983.
383. "Alice Theresa Hribal/Dodge," Ancestry.com, 2020, https://www.ancestry.com/family-tree/person/tree/6521211/person/-643573430/facts.
384. "US Social Security Death Index, 1935–2014—Mildred Grant," Ancestry.com, accessed July 14, 2022.
385. "John H. Larson," Martin Schwartz Funeral Homes & Crematory, February 28, 2012, http://obitarchive.martinschwartzfuneralhomes.tributecenteronline.com/Archived%20Obituaries_Services,%20L-Lk.html.
386. "Loyal D. Lubach," CHT, December 28, 2001.
387. "Benjamin Albert 'Benny' Smith," Find a Grave, 2010, https://www.findagrave.com/memorial/92620433/benjamin-a-smith.
388. "Earl R. White," CHT, April 6, 2002.
389. "SSGT Mortimer C. Anderson," Find a Grave, 2010, https://www.findagrave.com/memorial/110144677/mortimer-c-anderson.
390. Selden, interview.
391. "Mrs. Ualia Webb," CHT, June 9, 1945.
392. "1005 Warren Street—Kramer," CHT, July 17, 1948.
393. "Harry B. MacRae Gives Christian Science Lecture," CHT, March 3, 1952.
394. "Gold Star Mothers," CHT, August 29, 1952.

395. "Kramer's Honored Golden Wedding Anniversary," CHT, April 6, 1960.

396. "Army Pvt. Gerald R. Kramer," CHT, November 3, 1959.

397. "David Kramer Obituary," Hartson Funeral Home, April 2022, https://www.legacy.com/us/obituaries/name/david-kramer-obituary?id=34652168.

398. "Father Glad Yellowstone Trip Preceded Son's Sacrifice for US at Pearl Harbor," Northern Pacific Railroad Bulletin, n.d., personal collection of John E. Kinville.

399. "Obituary—Ralph B. Kramer," CHT, December 2, 1966.

400. "Thrift Sale," CHT, April 5, 1967.

401. "Realtor Bob Kleinheinz Advertisement," CHT, May 23, 1967.

402. "Mrs. Ralph Kramer—Obituary," CHT, April 8, 1968.

403. "Robert L. Kramer—Obituary," CHT, August 14, 1995.

404. "Elsie M. Grip," Find a Grave, November 2016, https://www.findagrave.com/memorial/173033668/elsie-m-grip.

405. Annie Kramer, phone interview by John E. Kinville, July 26, 2022.

406. Ibid.

407. Ibid.

408. "Harry W. Kramer Wooden Plaque," March 31, 1942, personal collection of John E. Kinville.

409. "USS California—World War II Fact Sheet."

Appendix

410. Nimitz, telegram to Kramer.

411. Harry Wellington Kramer, "Hand-Written USS California Ship's Log," 1940–41, personal collection of John E. Kinville.

ABOUT THE AUTHOR

Author at the gravesite of Harry Kramer, National Memorial Cemetery of the Pacific, Honolulu, Hawaii, 2017. *Author's collection.*

John E. Kinville is a local historian who teaches American government at Chippewa Falls Senior High School. His first book, *The Grey Eagles of Chippewa Falls: A Hidden History of a Women's Ku Klux Klan in Wisconsin* (2020) was voted a "Best Local Book Released in the Last Year" in *VolumeOne* magazine's "Best of the Chippewa Valley" award series. He earned his BA in Broadfield Social Studies Education at the University of Wisconsin–Eau Claire and MA in history education at the University of Wisconsin–River Falls. Kinville is also a founder of Flags 4 the Fallen (www.flags4thefallen.org), an educational organization designed to honor his school's fallen American soldiers. He resides near Chippewa Falls with his wife, children and four cats. He can be reached directly by visiting his website, www.johnkinville.com.